I SHOULD HAVE BEEN MORE CAREFUL

Woody —
where have you been? Have not seen you in ages.

Pogo

ALSO BY THE AUTHOR:

John D. Echeverria, Pope Barrow, and Richard Roos-Collins, *Rivers at Risk* (Island Press, 1989).

I SHOULD HAVE BEEN MORE CAREFUL

POPE BARROW

Copyright © 2023 Pope Barrow.

All rights reserved. No part of this book may be used or reproduced by any means, graphic, electronic, or mechanical, including photocopying, recording, taping or by any information storage retrieval system without the written permission of the author except in the case of brief quotations embodied in critical articles and reviews.

Archway Publishing books may be ordered through booksellers or by contacting:

Archway Publishing
1663 Liberty Drive
Bloomington, IN 47403
www.archwaypublishing.com
844-669-3957

Because of the dynamic nature of the Internet, any web addresses or links contained in this book may have changed since publication and may no longer be valid. The views expressed in this work are solely those of the author and do not necessarily reflect the views of the publisher, and the publisher hereby disclaims any responsibility for them.

Any people depicted in stock imagery provided by Getty Images are models, and such images are being used for illustrative purposes only. Certain stock imagery © Getty Images.

ISBN: 978-1-6657-3694-7 (sc)
ISBN: 978-1-6657-3695-4 (hc)
ISBN: 978-1-6657-3693-0 (e)

Library of Congress Control Number: 2023900581

Print information available on the last page.

Archway Publishing rev. date: 01/25/2023

These stories are dedicated to my father, M. Pope Barrow, Sr.,
a consummate raconteur who taught me
that fun and adventure open the door to a good life.

CONTENTS

Acknowledgement xi
Introduction xiii

Chapter 1	**The Fun Started Early** 1
	Life and Death on the Farm 1
	Dealing with a Dangerous Outlaw 5
	Mentoring 11
	Guns and Vehicles...15
	For the Love of Speed 17
	Run Like the Wind 19
Chapter 2	**Teenage Escapades**... 23
	The Underpants Caper.. 23
	Alcohol Is Not Your Friend 26
Chapter 3	**Cars and Motorcycles** 29
	Motorcycles I Have Loved (and Lost)...................29
	How to Destroy a Perfectly Good Car 34
Chapter 4	**College and Law School**..................................... 38
	Rebel without a Cause 38
	King of the Moon.. 40
	Abandoned at Vassar.. 44
	The Great Gatsby 46
	What's Next?... 48
Chapter 5	**An Irresponsible Young Adult** 51
	Party Games 51
	The View from the Tree 53

Chapter 6	**Hitting the Road**..57	
	Where's Henry?...57	
	A Hick from Maryland Does Not Belong in	
	North Africa...62	
	Lost White Boy in Search of Enlightenment...............68	
	Too Deep in the Jungle......................................76	
	Acapulco Gold..78	
	Baja California..81	
	The Last of the Big-Wave Body Surfers.........................85	
	The Dog Ate My Passport..................................88	
Chapter 7	**Kayaking Adventures—and Misadventures**............91	
	Free Falling: No Mistakes Allowed 91	
	The Last Steak 95	
	Fear Can Be Your Friend: A Short Essay 101	
	Disaster Averted at the Gauley Fest....................104	
	Pigs with Horns..108	
Chapter 8	**We Be Sailin', Mon** 111	
	We Were Damn Lucky....................................111	
	Sailing with a Scaredy-Cat................................119	
	Captain Runaground..125	
	The Potato 128	
	Chased By Bulls in the Azores 134	
	Captains Courageous 136	
	Sailboat Racing on the Chesapeake (Are We	
	Having Fun Yet?)..140	
	Close Call on the Dreaded C&D Canal...............144	
Chapter 9	**It Was Not All Fun** 148	
	Cousin Arthur..148	
	Fear and Loathing at Lisbon Elementary 149	
	Behind Bars..153	
	A Betrayal of Trust..158	
	Swimming with Sharks....................................162	
	Marriages and Divorces 167	
	Frog-Walked Out of the White House 175	
	A Very Bad Day..178	

Chapter 10 The Comedies of Old Age **180**
               The Cookie Monster...180
               When Everything Gets Old..182
               The Emperor of All Maladies...184
               My Last Big Adventure...186

Epilogue   Memory, Truth, Fiction, and Reality..............................191
               Unreliable Perceptions 192
               Flawed Recall.. 196
               Postmodern Philosophy..198
               Quantum Physics and Schrödinger's Cat.....................198
               Psychedelic Experiences.. 199
About the Author 201

ACKNOWLEDGEMENT

This little volume would have emerged a lot earlier, and would have been a total mess, if not for the expertise of my skilled editor and loving partner, Amber Jones. She dedicated countless hours of her retirement years to the project of cleaning up my language and punctuation as well as ensuring the stories make sense.

Despite the misery of having to confront my shortcomings as an author, I am eternally grateful to her for her efforts to make this book readable.

INTRODUCTION

As you get older, three things happen. The first is your memory goes, and I can't remember the other two.
—Sir Norman Wisdom

The author-undertaker Thomas Lynch once wrote that the one thing death can't steal is our stories.[1] That is not correct, because if you don't sing your own songs before you die, someone else may do it. And you might not like how they sound.

Even worse, your stories could disappear.

So I decided to write down some of the stories I love to tell so that death can't steal them.

My father made it clear to me as a young boy that it was important to enjoy life and have fun. It might, in fact, be the most important thing in life. He never said so explicitly, but observing how he lived, it was obvious that fun was at the center of the chaos.

Most of the stories in this little volume describe the ways in which I relentlessly searched for more fun—and the consequences thereof. Some of my escapades were inspired. Some were ridiculous. Some worked out well. Some did not. There was sometimes a bit of risk involved in trying to have a good time, especially if you like doing the kinds of things I liked to do.

Playing around and having fun seems a frivolous goal. What good are you doing for mankind? For the planet? On the other hand, if you are miserable all the time, it's going to be hard to save the planet or

---

[1] Thomas Lynch, "What Takes Our Breath Away," *The Atlantic*, June 2020.

achieve anything else. No one is going to want to help you with it, for one thing.

Seeking a good time as a way of life may seem to be a bit of an ego trip, but it is not completely without philosophical support. Decrying the modern obsession with work, Bertrand Russell said that without leisure "a man is cut off from the best things."[2] Immanuel Kant tied it into enlightenment, overthrowing the bonds of conformity, censorship, and the burdensome rules of society.

Recent research backs the importance of fun. In her book, the science journalist Catherine Price points to some convincing studies that suggest that fun is important to health and happiness. She isolated the three essential elements involved in having the kind of fun that leads to good results: rebel and be playful, connect with people, and be present in the flow.[3]

I have not always nailed the trifecta, but, in my life, I have very often nailed the first element.

And I sometimes paid the price.

---

[2] Bertrand Russell, "In Praise of Idleness," *Harper's Magazine,* October 1932.
[3] Catherine Price, *The Power of Fun: How to be Alive Again* (Dial Press, 2021).

1

THE FUN STARTED EARLY

LIFE AND DEATH ON THE FARM

Early in life I began my relentless quest for adventure and fun, accompanied by the unfortunate consequences of this search.

I lived on a dairy farm in Maryland. This offered abundant opportunities for lots of fun and also opportunities for risky, stupid behavior; questionable choices; and catastrophic accidents.

My frazzled mother's idea of child rearing was to announce to her three hyperactive young boys, as we ran around the house breaking fragile items and knocking pictures off the wall, "You boys go outside and help your father. We will ring the bell when it's time to eat."

The bell was a big iron monster mounted on two tall wooden posts outside the kitchen door of the main farmhouse. You could hear it ring from far away. My mother and her cook used it at lunchtime to call in the people working at the barn or out in the fields (and the children running amok somewhere in the woods) at lunchtime.

Our family farmhouse

My mother's vague instructions about "going outside" opened up 300 acres of adventures and trouble. The possibilities to screw up were endless. My two younger brothers and I had fields to roam, trees to climb, tall windmills to fall from, snakes and other wild creatures to play with. One of my brothers fell out of a barn door and broke his arm. I broke my fingers and arm and had several teeth knocked out. Cuts, broken bones, animal bites, and bee stings were routine.

This kind of unsupervised mayhem set up a pattern for later life—a pattern rife with reckless behavior and risky activities, often ending in injuries. The common denominator was the endless quest for fun.

Ours was a hard-scrabble, labor-intensive dairy farm, which my father drove into bankruptcy. Several times. I lived there until I was 16. These days almost no one grows up on a real working farm like ours. In my stuffy Ivy League college, when I mentioned that I lived on a farm, my classmates were baffled. To them, a farm was a place where one kept their polo ponies. But one does not live there.

Farm life in those days was a far cry from city or suburban life. My companions were domestic and wild animals, cows, horses, dogs, pigs, goats, sheep, chickens, foxes, ducks, birds, snakes, groundhogs, pheasants, wasps, bees, other insects of all kinds, turtles, and fish. And of course my siblings, who were available to fight with. Night life was owls hooting, frogs croaking, and lightning bugs flashing.

As companions, animals can, in many ways, be superior to humans. The domesticated ones are not hostile, critical, or suspicious. You can hold them and pet them. All they want from you is food and protection. Best of all, they seldom, if ever, lie to you or reject your companionship.

We had three dogs, Champ, Tippy, and Nippy. I also had a pet duck that I took to the county fair where he won a prize. We also had calves, a pony, and two horses. Although our farm was a dairy farm, we had added pigs, chickens, and a few strong-smelling goats.

Our chickens were beautiful, dressed in colorful feathers. They came in dozens of varieties and several colors. We always had plenty of eggs. As a child, I fed the chickens and collected eggs. I always thought the chickens must love me because they were always following me around, clucking affectionately.

Chickens love me

Wild animals were even more exciting. Possums. Buzzards. Skunks. Snakes. Raccoons. Tadpoles. And snails. You could find a black snake within minutes of walking out the front door. If you were quiet and still, you could watch the foxes, deer, hummingbirds, and bluegills in the pond. Swimming in the pond was always a thrill, especially given the frequent sightings there of water moccasins and huge snapping turtles. Another thrill was to whack wasp nests with a stick and try to run for it before they stung you. That seldom ended well.

One year, my father gave me a newborn calf for Christmas. I fed and raised the calf, won prizes with him at the county fair, and spent a lot of time petting and grooming him. He was an awesome companion. Eventually, he turned into a big healthy steer.

One day my steer was nowhere to be found. I searched everywhere. My parents responded to my questions with an uneasy silence. Then it dawned on me. While I was away at school, my beloved pet had been taken to the stockyard at Slacks Corner where a butcher transformed him into hamburgers, steak, and roast beef. It was a sad revelation about how things worked.

Obviously, not everything was idyllic, fun, and beautiful in my childhood. Not only did pets become food. Pigs got slaughtered and hung up behind the back porch with their eyeballs rolling around the back yard. It wasn't so much fun for the chickens, either, when it was their turn. My father would cut off a chicken's head with a hatchet on the back stairs. The headless bird would then stumble for a surprisingly long time around the yard, blood squirting from its neck all over the yard, until it flopped over in a final convulsion.

Dinner.

It was always poignant when any chicken met its final end because I fed them and knew each individual chicken. They had names. It might be Helen, Frida, Jezebel, or another friend of mine out there running around headless. It turned out to be a mistake to get too attached to chickens, calves, and ducks. It's easier these days, when the only animals I meet are in plastic packages at the grocery store.

DEALING WITH A DANGEROUS OUTLAW

Any story can be revisited, recast, and even remade.
—Rachel Syme, "Fool Me Once," *The New Yorker*, October 19, 2020

My 3-year-old brother was up on a chair, under a big tree limb out on our lawn. A noose was around his neck, with the rope up over the tree limb. I was trying to push the chair out from under him. I was almost 5 years old at the time.

How did this dire situation evolve?

One of my earliest memories is sitting in the swing on the side front porch at our family farm with my grandfather in the evening. We watched the sunset as the day gradually gave way to night. Owls were hooting faintly. Then my grandfather would turn on the radio as he sipped a small glass of bourbon and water. He was a county judge, and he loved the sound of the owls and the radio stories about crime and the Wild West. That was back in the 1940s. As a 4- and 5-year old, my imagination about the Wild West was on fire.

One of the shows we listened to was *Gunsmoke*, with U.S. Marshal Matt Dillon. Even today, every Sunday night at 8:00 pm, I listen to *Gunsmoke* on a public radio station that plays old-time radio dramas.

My brothers and I entertained ourselves on the farm in different ways than city kids did. There was no TV; instead, we had radio, comic books, and occasional movies in town. Otherwise, most of our playtime was outdoors. Indoors we broke china, furniture, and other vulnerable things while relentlessly roughhousing.

The games we played relied on radio shows, early movies, and our imaginations. The scenes were in the fields and woods. The other actors were farm animals, wild animals, ponies, and horses.

There was, in those days, what passed for a makeshift movie theater in the nearby little rural village of Sykesville. It was only a room above the bank, with a crappy little screen set up on one wall and folding chairs.

The bank building in Sykesville

We saw lots of classic black and white films in the Sykesville theater. We saw the original *King Kong* movie there. (They were not "classics" then, of course; they were new releases.) My brother, Henry, hid on the floor behind the chairs during the scary parts of *King Kong*. He kept asking me, "Is it over yet?"

When they started making movies in color, we had to go about 20 miles to a larger town, Damascus. A real theater there offered Technicolor movies. I recently passed through Damascus. The theater is now closed, like so many others in rural areas.

We saw a lot of westerns. *Shane* with Alan Ladd and Jack Palance was a favorite. Of course, there were often hangings in the old westerns. That was a good way to get rid of the bad guys. The other way, of course, was to shoot them down in a gun fight.

One day, with our imaginations fueled by those movies, Henry and I were playing cowboys and lawmen. It was one of our favorite games. The game involved a lot of running around hiding in "forts" and pretending to get shot, with lots of drama. The lawman always won, of course.

We had seen a bad guy getting hung by the neck in a movie. So I suggested to Henry that we finish our game with a western-style hanging. Henry went along with the idea. We scoured the farm to find a rope and attempted to tie some kind of loop in it. Then we dragged a chair out in the yard under a big tree limb.

When it came time to decide who was going to get hung and who was going to do the hanging, there was no dispute. In our family there was a clear seniority system. Henry was younger and below me in the pecking order. Our youngest brother, Jake, had not yet been born. Soon, he would take his place at the absolute bottom of the pecking order, above only our dogs, Tippy, Nippy, and Champ.

Up onto the chair went the bad guy, Henry, with the noose around his neck. Somehow I got the rope over the tree limb. Things were looking good for a hanging, at least if you were me, the lawman. Not so good if you were what the cowboys called a "pesky varmint."

Unbeknownst to us, someone was watching as we put this drama together. My mother's cook and housekeeper, Marie Hammond, saw what was about to take place. Marie had been ironing clothes at the side door of the kitchen. She dropped the iron and came running out of the kitchen door, screaming at me to stop immediately. She lifted Henry down off the chair and took the noose off his neck.

A savior had intervened in our lives. Her quick action prevented my overactive imagination from leading to a possible murder.

In Ancient Greek theater, playwrights used a device called (in Latin) the *deus ex machina*. Roughly translated, the phrase means "a god from a machine." The hero of the Greek play would get himself in a bad fix. If the playwright could not figure out how to work out a good ending, out of nowhere came the *deus ex machina*. It was a big machine that arose from beneath the stage containing one or more of the Greek gods. The god or gods made a little speech and saved the hero. It was a cheap plot device, but Greek audiences loved it.

Henry and I were saved by a *deus ex machina*, in the shape of Marie Hammond.

In fact, I owe many lucky escapes in my life to the fortuitous intervention of a *deus ex machina* who stepped in to save me from the consequences of my decisions.

Over my 80 years of pursuing fun activities, I often wound up in a bad fix. Out of the blue, a *deus ex machina*—my mother, a worker on our farm, a close friend, a schoolmate, a rescue boat captain, or some astute anonymous Good Samaritan—rescued me. Marie Hammond was one of the first.

The hanging incident proved to be the beginning of an alarming pattern in my life—one that repeated itself throughout my childhood, adolescence, early adulthood, and on into old age. The pattern consists of four stages:

1. Try to have as much fun and excitement as possible without regard to obvious dangers.
2. In search of that goal, do something stupid or dangerous.
3. Be fortunate enough to have someone else save me from the consequences of the stupid behavior.
4. Repeat the pattern in a new and even more hazardous context.

Various versions of the *deus ex machina* had their work cut out for them throughout my life.

The hanging incident also could be part of the reason why my brother Henry, to this day, has a hard time trusting me. He still suspects that I don't have his welfare as my first priority.

After the sibling hanging was fortuitously foiled by Marie Hammond, my father ordered me to go "to the pump house"—another prominent feature of life on the farm, and one that was no fun at all. The pump house was the basement of a small building also referred to as the "meat house." We stored hams in the top of this damp and moldy shed while they cured. Down below in the quiet, musty, cold stone basement of that building, we received our richly deserved corporeal punishments.

The pump house at our farm

For a serious offense, my father, a Marine Corps veteran, brought into service an instrument we knew as the "Marine Corps belt." It was a heavy canvas belt with a metal buckle. For some reason, we feared this belt more than any other instrument of punishment.

Before the Marine Corps belt appeared, our father used a paddle stored in the rafters of the pump house. On one occasion, we decided to get rid of the dreaded paddle. We threw it out into the field. Enter the much worse Marine Corps belt.

We stuffed paper and comic books into the back of our pants to blunt the pain, but Dad was on to that trick. Before the whipping started, he would always say: "Take down your pants!" All the papers and comic books would fall out.

I got the Marine Corps belt on my butt numerous times the night after the attempted hanging. I suspected that Henry probably lay in bed laughing while I was suffering in the pump house.[4]

---

[4] Of course, Henry's memory varies significantly from mine regarding the incident with the noose. He claims: "I did not suggest this terribly dangerous

The worst thing about getting punished as a little kid was not the pain. It was the anticipation. The psychological torture. My dad would send us to the pump house and tell us to wait for him there. The waiting was horrible. We panicked. We considered running away from home. We considered hiding in the woods. We considered pleading our case and begging. Our anxiety grew and grew. Sometimes he would leave us there, suffering and in fear, for a good long time. He never much relished administering the whippings, but probably did not know what else to do once he had set things in motion.

My father
Photo credit: Tom Wolfe

We stayed in that pump house scared out of our wits until our dad finally showed up. It was almost a relief when the actual whipping began. His heart was never in it and it never hurt all that much. Certainly nowhere near as much as we imagined it would.

On one occasion we actually did run away from home in terror, to avoid the whipping. We stayed out in the woods until late at night

---

game; it was mandated by Pope. I was punished as well as Pope, because our dad (always with his incredible lack of fair jurisprudence) preferred not to cast blame, but he instead simply punished all involved."

before creeping back home. That changed things somehow. We got no more whippings after that.

MENTORING

As the firstborn in my family of three brothers, I was entitled to certain privileges. I also had certain obligations.

One of my obligations was to guide and mentor the other two little laggards. I knew the score, and they did not. Believe me, those little miscreants badly needed guidance, especially at their earlier ages... before they became rebellious.

Mentoring is an important skill to learn. The world is full of confused people who need guidance. I always stand ready to help them. Especially if there is something in it for me.

The birth of my first brother, Henry, was a thrill for me. Here was some red meat I could turn into a companion for all sorts of activities on the farm. I would have a sidekick to do with me all the fun stuff a kid can do in the country: build tree houses; catch snakes and snapping turtles; shoot squirrels, chipmunks and groundhogs; catch bluegills; chase cows around; and, most importantly, do my chores for me.

I realized that it would be much more fun to have a mentee to do dangerous stuff with. With a junior scout, and me as the senior scout, I would not have to approach the copperhead snake, wasp nest, or snapping turtle myself. I could coach him how to do it while I kept a safe distance, ready to run like hell.

As soon as Henry leaned to walk, I began mentoring him. There were a few hiccups, such as the attempted hanging mentioned in the previous story. But generally, I thought he was coming along well. One of the most important things a mentor must teach his mentee is how to stand up for himself and not get taken advantage of. The way you teach this is to abuse the crap out of the mentee until he finally wises up and, like you, becomes a monster in his own right.

One of my favorite techniques was to trick the trusting and naïve mentee into doing my chores for me. You promise the mentee gifts and rewards if he does the chore. You can promise something you know he wants—candy, marbles, a live bug from your collection. All he has to do, for example, is go down to the barn and carry a heavy can of milk back to the house in a freezing snowstorm. After he does the miserable chore (which was originally assigned by parents to you), you neglect to come through with the promised reward.

Depending on how young and gullible the mentee is, you can sometimes pull this one off repeatedly.

This exercise teaches the mentee an important lesson. You cannot trust con men and scam artists, especially those in your own family.

If the mentor fails to show some restraint, mentoring can sometimes go off the tracks. The classic case in my life was the disturbing hamburger incident.

Our parents went out to a cocktail party, which they were always doing back in those days. My instructions were to take care of my younger brother. Feed him dinner and stuff like that. I was pretty puffed up about this huge responsibility and took it very seriously. I was the boss of the house now.

I cooked Henry a hamburger and put pickles, mustard, and ketchup on it. I ordered him to sit his puny little ass down at the kitchen table and eat what I put in front of him. He took one look at the hamburger and said, "I ain't eating that crap. I hate ketchup." I told him angrily, "Listen here, you little twerp, you are going to eat that hamburger or else."

Henry has had a stubborn streak since the earliest age. My parents considered him to be "ornery." On one occasion my father told him that he had to eat his lima beans before he could go to bed. Henry refused. I still recall my amazement when I came downstairs the next morning. Henry was still sitting at the table in front of an untouched plate of lima beans.

I was frustrated that Henry would not eat the beautiful hamburger I had struggled so hard to make for him. The stubborn little bastard flatly refused. And I was not going to humiliate myself by begging.

So I took the bun off the top of the hamburger. Then, I placed the hamburger, dripping with ketchup and mustard, in my right hand. I reared back and pressed it firmly into his face, ketchup and mustard and all. Then I ground it in a bit.

Henry sat there quietly for a moment, ketchup and mustard draining down his face onto his lap. Finally he said quietly, "Pope. I am going to kill you." At that moment, I knew my mentoring had succeeded. Maybe a bit too well.

Henry stood up, went over to the kitchen drawer, and got out a knife. I knew he was deadly serious.

I took off at high speed out through the kitchen door and ran around the other side of the house. He was after me and not kidding around. I went into hiding until our parents got home. At that point, I tried to rat him out, but the usual punishment ensued.

My dad was not into listening to whining, whimpering, crying, excuse-making, or judicial arguments about who did what and who was innocent and who was guilty. He simply beat the crap out of everyone involved. We both got a good beating that night.

After that incident, I never again felt the need to mentor my brother Henry. He had learned the main lesson: "Don't take any crap from anyone." Actually, I was kind of intimidated by him after that. I guess that is what successful mentoring is all about.

Although Henry had outgrown the need for my guidance, my youngest brother, Jake, at age 4, still needed my help. I thought he should learn some survival skills, and, as an experienced 7-year-old, I was the best person to teach him.

Our parents did not believe in allowances. Or perhaps they were too broke all the time to spare a little cash for us kids. This meant that, if we wanted candy or comic books, or anything else that cost money, we needed an alternative way to acquire these desirable objects.

In the absence of an allowance, I decided that shoplifting would be the preferred method of acquiring things we lusted after. Shoplifting is a survival skill that all young children without any cash flow need to learn at an early age. There was a side benefit for the mentor as well. The proceeds of the enterprise (candy bars, chewing gum, comic books, and other items) would naturally have to be split with the mentor.

I explained to Jake how a skilled shoplifter works. We started at McDougall's pharmacy in Sykesville. In that store, candy and a huge assortment of other goodies sat in front of the counter. Easy pickings. I told Jake to grab as much as he could get in his pockets. Then he was to hightail it out of the store. Meanwhile, I distracted the druggist with idiotic fake questions.

The scam would have worked, but Jake was too small to reach most of the desirable items. He was also dropping stuff on the floor and generally being way too obvious.

That evening, the pharmacist, Dr. McDougall, called our mother. He reported the failed theft and fingered Jake as the perp. Jake had to go in the store and eat crow. Meanwhile I laid low.

Not all mentees are good students. Jake was a total failure at shoplifting in his early years. But much later in life, in college, he became extremely proficient. Maybe my early efforts were not for naught after all.

As is so often the case with my memories, Jake recalls the incident in a slightly different way. His version shows some imaginative distortions and embellishments of the true facts I have accurately reported above.[5] His version brings to mind the saying: "The older I get, the more clearly I remember things that never happened."

---

[5] Jake's version goes as follows: "We had this scam going for quite a while. Stealing comic books like Mad Magazine was a particular reward. It was working out pretty well until Dr. McDougall began to notice slipping inventory or something fishy going on. His suspicions led him to call our mother on the telephone (157J party line) and ask that she investigate the possibility of her good boys taking things without paying. In our family, it would be unthinkable that the grandsons of Judge Forsythe would purposefully steal anything. One night while I was in my bedroom right over the kitchen, mother called in Pope for a face-to-face interrogation. I was listening through the floor boards to the conversation. When the theft subject came up, Pope realized that he had only two choices. Come completely clean and tell the whole story or lie his way out

GUNS AND VEHICLES

Kids and guns are not a good mix, but we begged for guns when I was a young kid. Guns looked like incredible fun; they were also a symbol of privilege and maturity. We begged ourselves into possession of shotguns and .22-caliber rifles as soon as we were big enough to lift them. We shot almost every wild animal that moved. Nothing was safe around our farm. Not birds, not chipmunks, not groundhogs, not squirrels, and not turtles.

We may have felt privileged, but we were far from mature. It was not unheard of for one brother to get shot by a BB gun owned by another brother. I shot my youngest brother in the arm with a BB gun to prevent him from trespassing into my secret fort. He got his revenge, however. He ratted me out to our father. I lost my BB gun because of that.

We were lucky that none of us three boys got shot with our own .22 rifles. A 10-year-old friend of ours was not so lucky. David Zeeveld managed to shoot himself in the head while cleaning his supposedly unloaded rifle. (He is now paralyzed.)

Playing with real guns offered a lot of room for stupid mistakes, but farm machines were the bigger and more dangerous attractions. Bailers. Saws. Mowers. The big greasy iron stuff, with shiny blades and

---

of it. He excelled in the art of lying. Pope was never too good at coming clean, so he opted for the second approach. He put the whole thing on me, proclaimed his own innocence, and professed knowing nothing about it but wondering how I came out of the store with so much candy, gum, etc.

Pope made it perfectly clear to mother that I couldn't be trusted and would probably lie my way out of the situation, and it would be important to teach me a lesson. Pope was released from cross-examination and returned to his room.

The next day it was announced that I was the thief and was going to have to go to the pharmacy and apologize to Dr. McDougall. I was going to take the fall. Pope felt that this was a much better way to resolve touchy issues than to have to get personally involved. He would remember this lesson well into adulthood. Meanwhile Pope laid low, and we all avoided stealing from McDougall's until some safe period of time had passed. There were other stores in Sykesville with plenty of offerings and supplies that we needed."

whirling choppers. Long before I started school, I decided I wanted to be a farmer like my dad. Most of all, I dreamed of driving his alluring, bright green John Deere tractor. Once, when dad was nowhere in sight, I got on the tractor. I was too small to reach the pedals or the gears, but the key was in the ignition. I climbed up on the tractor seat. I got it started and in gear. This is going to be cool! I thought.

The tractor went straight through the barn wall with me perched atop before I discovered how to stop it.

Even away from the farm, I managed to stumble into vehicular trouble. I was about 4 years old when my mother drove me to Ellicott City, Maryland. She parked her Willys Jeep Wagon on the steep hill of Main Street, leaving me alone in the front seat. She ran off on a quick errand. Mother was never terribly obsessed with child safety, and this was long before seat belts and child seats. Bored stiff waiting around alone in the car, I decided to do what big people did.

I got behind the wheel and somehow got the car in neutral with the brake off. Driving Mom's car looked like a lot of fun to a 4-year-old! But to a guy walking by on the sidewalk, it looked like a runaway car with no driver. I was too short to see or be seen through the window. The car began rolling slowly down the steep hill. Luckily, the observant Good Samaritan jumped into the car and hit the brakes before we accelerated down that long steep slope toward oblivion.

Trying to drive a car while 4 years old was not my best idea. But it was a preview of my fun-seeking life to come. Often I have nearly killed myself or someone else by making a reckless move or brainless mistake. Then, out of the blue, some lucky thing happened, or some other person—a *deus ex machina*, like that man on Main Street—intervened.

In particular, my transition from farm life—with all of its temptations and exciting opportunities for fun and dangerous adventures—to city life as an older teenager was not easy. I always wanted to make a run for it, go somewhere different, or do something wild, unpredictable, and fun. This quest led to many questionable decisions, some serious injuries, and numerous disasters. It also presented opportunities for others to save my butt.

FOR THE LOVE OF SPEED

One of the things I became enraptured with—one might say addicted to—as a young boy growing up was speed. At first it was riding horses as fast as they could go. Pure excitement. That experience led to the pony cart disaster.

We had a black and white pony named Tommy and a wicker two-wheeled cart that Tommy could be hitched up to. The idea my mother had was that we would cruise gently and slowly around the fields and farm roads in this ridiculous antique contraption, spreading joy and goodwill, just as she had done with her well-dressed girlfriends when she was a little girl in fancy clothes.

It did not work out that way. I was already addicted to speed by the time we got Tommy pulling the cart. The idea of modestly cruising around like little gentlemen was not what I had in mind. I was thinking of other, more exciting possibilities, such as: "How fast can we get this old buggy going?"

After hitching up Tommy, feeding him a few Lucky Strike cigarettes (which he consumed like candy), and walking him with the cart slowly around the yard to impress our mother, my brother Henry and I decided to take things further afield and unsupervised. An old little-used farm road, out of sight of the main house, connected several fields. It joined Forsythe Road to Old Frederick Road. It looked to us like a good race track, even though it was an old, rocky dirt road buried between two high embankments. We drove the pony cart, with Tommy pulling, over to this road to see how fast Tommy could pull the fragile cart.

It turned out that Tommy could go very fast indeed. When whipped on his rear with a leather horse whip, he took off like a bolt of lightning.

We dubbed the old road "The Speedaway." It was where we would go every chance we got and get Tommy running like hell, with the rickety cart crashing along behind him, and us bouncing up and down and holding on for dear life. It was about the most fun that two young boys could possibly have.

These wild escapades went on for a while until, on one reckless speed test, a wheel came off the cart. Henry and I went flying through the air. We crash-landed in the adjacent field. Henry was beat up pretty bad. That was the end of the pony cart speed trials. The vehicle did not survive the crash.

There were still other speed trials to do, however. A short steep hill led down to the farm's front entrance, followed by a longer series of hills going all the way down to the bottomland and stream. It was about a half mile of downhill road. If you perched on your bike at the top of the first hill and pedaled as hard as you could, you could fly down that hill at an uncontrollable speed. You would flash around a blind curve, hoping that nothing was coming the other way.

That hill was a thrill never to be forgotten. Eventually it led to even more extreme efforts to feed the speed addiction, using motorcycles and cars.

More about those vehicles later. As for understanding the thrill of speed, I learned a lot about that later in life from Ken Knowles. Ken was a blind British sailor who was sailing his own sailboat across the Atlantic Ocean for the second time when I joined him. On that trip, I acted as his eyes. I did my best to steer his boat safely into some rocky, ridiculously inaccessible, and treacherous harbors in the Azores.

Ken explained to me that he never wanted to be limited to a dull and boring life merely because he was blind. When he was a young lad in England, he attended a school for blind boys. They may have been sight-impaired, but these boys were 100% male. They had a wild streak, and Ken was the leader of the pack. The boys discovered some sleds around the school buildings. When the snow came, they snuck out to the steep hill behind the school and took off downhill at top speed on the sleds. At first they didn't know there was a road at the bottom. None of the wild and crazy little blind boys ever got run over, but motorists freaked out. The boys got caught and lost their sleds to the school authorities. Ken said that was his first taste of exciting adventure. He was addicted.

Close your eyes and imagine in your mind that you are flying on a sled or a pair of skis down a steep snowy hill. You are completely blind. That might give you a feel for what the thrill of speed is all about. An American Olympian, Mike May, was blinded at age 3 yet took up competitive skiing at age 27. He once hit 65 mph in a competition and said, "It was extremely liberating."[6]

My own love of speed was deep and long-lasting. It led to some ugly consequences, all of which I survived—barely.

RUN LIKE THE WIND

I ground my heels into the horse's side and prodded him into a fast gallop. I panicked. My heartbeat was racing. I galloped up the dirt lane to Nick Hammond's farmhouse and jumped off. I ran up the porch steps and banged on the door, yelling "Mrs. Hammond! Come quick! Mr. Hammond got hurt. It's bad!"

Mrs. Hammond, after what seemed an eternity, came to the door and said, "What happened? What are you doing here?"

Breathing hard, I gasped: "I was riding down your lane and I saw Mr. Hammond on the ground in the field. He was next to the tractor and mower and the tractor was still running. He said to call for help. He was bleeding. He cut his foot off!"

This was one of the many adventures I encountered while riding horses. Sometimes, I got lucky and the adventure didn't end in disaster—at least not for me.

When I was growing up on the farm in Maryland, the area where we lived was still horse country. There were horse shows at the old Carroll place down the road, Doreghan Manor, and at stables all

---

[6] May holds the record for downhill skiing by a person who is completely blind. He competed in the 1984 Winter Paralympics.

around. Everyone on the other farms (the Royer and the Hernandez farms, especially) had horses, and so did we. Being a little kid around those huge powerful animals was one of the coolest things about farm life.

When I was 4 or 5 years old, we started out with small ponies. Tommy was the black and white one. Tommy was not trained as a riding pony. He hated saddles and would not respond well to signals from the rider. He always tried to bite the rider and buck him off. He could be tamed only briefly by giving him cigarettes to eat. He could eat a whole pack of Lucky Strikes lickety-split, filter and all.

Tommy had been trained to pull a buggy. As recounted in the previous story, my brother Henry and I would harness Tommy to a buggy. He would immediately take off and run like hell, sometimes resulting in disaster.

Later on we got two much larger horses, Jasper and Wartalk. Jasper was a retired polo pony. He was a full-size horse, but they called all the polo horses ponies. It was wild riding Jasper. With a tiny signal from a shift in my feet, he would wheel around on a dime and head off at top speed in the opposite direction, probably dreaming that he was chasing after an imaginary polo ball that he remembered from his competitive days.

I was crazy about riding Jasper. He loved to go fast, and it was a challenge to stay aboard. When no one else was around, although it was prohibited, I rode him bareback.

He had four speeds: walk, trot, gallop, and RUN LIKE THE WIND. It was easy to stay aboard walking, but not so easy trotting. Trotting was bumpy, and I tended to slide around on his back, with no saddle to grip on to. Galloping was a little better, but still bumpy. When I got Jasper in fourth gear riding bareback, however, it was transcendental. It was smooth and so incredibly fast that I could not believe it. The wind would be blowing my hair back, and I would have to lean forward, holding on with my arms around Jasper's neck. I felt like we were one single machine going as fast as possible. I was not allowed to do that, of course, but I did it all the time anyway and never got caught. I couldn't get enough of riding Jasper in fourth gear.

My younger brother, Henry, also got the horseback-riding bug. He even got a job exercising horses for a neighbor, the beautiful blond Mrs. Royer. That lasted until he got bucked off and fired.

One day, Henry threw a baseball at Jasper's face while I was in the saddle. Jasper reared up, and I fell off the saddle. Unfortunately, my foot got entangled in one of the stirrups. Jasper was running in fourth gear to get away from Henry, with me dangling by one leg, foot tangled in the stirrup. My head was frighteningly close to his hooves, almost bouncing off the ground.

My luck held this time. I was so short at that age that my head did not reach either the ground or Jasper's hooves. I survived until he came to a stop about a quarter of a mile away.

Interestingly, Henry says he does not remember any of this incident—offering proof that memories can be slippery. His, or mine?

I was riding Jasper to visit my friend Johnny Porter, passing through Nick Hammond's farm, when the incident occurred with Nick's cut foot. The route to Johnny Porter's farm went through Nick's farm and down his entrance lane.

While riding down that lane, I saw Nick's tractor in the field with the engine running, but no driver. It looked like he had been mowing hay with a large sharp blade that stuck out to the right side of the tractor. That blade was known as a "side sickle bar." Looking more closely, I saw Nick on the ground in front of the cutting blade, holding his leg.

Tractor with Sickle Cutting Blade

Nick's leg had been cut at the ankle and he was bleeding profusely. After I hurried to the house and found Mrs. Hammond, she called for an ambulance from Eldersburg. The ambulance came quickly and saved his life. But his foot was almost completely severed.

I don't know what would have happened had I not been riding by that afternoon. No one else was around. Nick Hammond may well have bled to death.

That incident may have been the only time in my life that I saved someone else from the bad consequences of a mistake they made! Usually, I was the one needing to be saved.

The way I see it, I made a deposit in the karma bank that day. Of course, I have been drawing down on that deposit ever since.

2

TEENAGE ESCAPADES

THE UNDERPANTS CAPER

> *It's life's illusions I recall.*
> —Joni Mitchell, "Both Sides Now," 1966

It's amazing what trivial little things can do for a person's reputation. When my brother Henry told some fellow construction workers that he had made a big sexual conquest the previous night, they did not believe him—until he convinced them to drive by the Howard County High School. As they drove by the school, Henry suggested they look at the flag pole out front. A pair of pink girl's underwear was flapping in the breeze from the top of the pole. That physical evidence firmly cemented Henry's reputation as a major ladies' man.

Living out in rural Howard County, Maryland, when my brothers and I were teenagers, meant constant plotting to escape the loneliness and boredom of farm life. We wanted to experience the wild times in the big city. The big city in those days was not Baltimore, the closest city, but Washington, D.C. The reason was that the drinking age in Maryland was 21; in Washington it was 18. This legal discrepancy resulted in pilgrimages to our D.C. Mecca as soon as we turned 18. The bars and nightclubs of Georgetown beckoned, and Maryland kids between 18 and 21 flooded into D.C. in droves every weekend.

Once we got possession of our parents' car, with solemn promises to go nowhere dangerous, it was "Katie bar the door!" I doubt our parents thought we were headed to a local church social, but they crossed their fingers and hoped for the best.

On one memorable occasion, I had a date with Beverly Davis. I had been chasing her for quite a while, and she consented to a trip to Georgetown with me. Her parents were none too pleased that she was going anywhere with me, with good reason. They took one look at me and concluded, "This kid is not going to be a good influence on Beverly." The fact that they disapproved is probably the main reason she was willing to go out with me.

Getting Beverly out of her house in Baltimore involved lots of parental warnings and threats accompanied by stern facial expressions. But I was a bad boy, just as they surmised, and once Beverly got in the car, it was PARTY TIME.

It was a double date. Henry's date was Heather Mason, who lived in the country near us. Henry had been trying unsuccessfully to get into Heather's underpants for as long as he had known her. She was a fiery, strong-willed, dark-haired beauty. Uncontrollable. Wild. It was impossible not to like her. She was funny and popular, but she had a crazy streak. You never knew what she was going to get up to when you were with her. She was always more unpredictable when drinking was involved.

The four of us headed to Georgetown to a joint called the Cellar Door on M Street, a famous watering hole and music venue which is now long gone. Henry and I were behind the joint at one point taking a pee in the alley when we were noticed by an elderly lady who had the misfortune to live right next to the club. There was some yelling back and forth. A brick was thrown and the cops were called. We went back in the club and stayed there until the police arrived to escort Henry out. Somehow he got the blame for the brick, but who knows who really was to blame. I am not sure why he was not carted off to jail, but the silver-tongued devil talked his way out of it.

By then it was very late. We had parental curfews to consider, but checking our watches, we realized that the deadlines were long gone. We were going to have to face the music at some point. But first we decided on a detour for some making out.

Our chosen venue was the Howard County High School near Heather's house. It was deserted at that time of night. Henry was still trying to make it with Heather, and I was probably doing the same with Beverly. Neither of us was having any success, but Henry finally did get Heather to at least take off her underpants, by promising to run them up the flag pole. This sounded to all of us like a fantastic idea. Once we had the underpants all the way up and admired our handiwork, we realized that there was no escape from the need to deliver the girls back home. No one was looking forward to that.

We took Heather home first, or tried to, but she was having an ornery moment and refused to get out of the car. It was getting really late now. We gave up on delivering Heather and all four of us drove to Baltimore, dropped Beverly off, and fled the premises. I don't know what Beverly's parents said to her when she got in, but I am sure that I was on their shit list forever after that.

The real challenge was to get Heather home before the sun came up. She definitely did not want to face her father, knowing she was going to get yelled at. We thought maybe we could sneak to her home and make a run for it like we had at Beverly's house. But Heather would still have to face the music, and she was having none of that. There was a long, forested entrance lane to the Masons' farmhouse, known as Squirrel Hill. It was a dirt road and we were creeping slowly up in the car, trying to be quiet.

When we neared the house, the first thing we saw was the menacing figure of Mr. Mason. Heather suddenly jumped out of the car and disappeared lickety-split, sneaking into the back of the house without saying a word to us or to her father.

Mr. Mason was standing on the porch. We did not see a shotgun, but he looked extremely unhappy. "Get up here, you boys," he growled. We were shaking in our boots. "I am calling your parents right now." That was good news to us because we feared our own parents a lot less than we feared an angry Jack Mason. The call was made, and we were sent home to face the music there.

I don't know what transpired in that conversation between the parents. We will never know because Jack Mason and our parents are all long gone now. Sadly, so is Heather. She died too young in a car accident.

We never told anyone other than the construction workers about the underpants caper. I don't think any of the parents would have appreciated the humor.

ALCOHOL IS NOT YOUR FRIEND

>*It was early last September*
>*As near as I remember*
>*While strolling down a lane in Riverside*
>
>*Not a soul was I disturbing*
>*While I lay there on the curbing*
>*When a pig came up and lay down by my side*
>
>*Not a word did we utter*
>*As we laid there in the gutter*
>*When this high-toned lass stopped by and I heard her say*
>*You can tell a man who boozes*
>*By the company he chooses*
>*And the pig got up and slowly walked away.*
>   —One of the versions of a Temperance-era song

Did I mention that alcohol was sometimes involved in the disastrous incidents in my young life?

One of my saviors was my high-school friend Henry Hopkins. There were multiple opportunities for him to perform this service, but this particular one found Henry, at 2 am, frantically ringing the doorbell at a doctor's office. Finally the sleeping doc woke up and came to the door. Henry explained that his friend had a little accident, and was cut to pieces. In fact he was in danger of bleeding to death. The doctor was not happy, but he took a look at me and said, "He needs a lot of stitches." So he sewed me up—without anesthesia. The doctor said, "I can smell his breath a mile away. He won't feel a thing." And I didn't. I don't remember if we even paid him for his troubles.

I awoke the next day with a legendary hangover, covered in a mass of stitches and bandages.

This incident happened when we were seniors in high school. The miscreants in my class, including me, took a spring break trip to Ocean City, Maryland. We piled into various cars and filled the trunks with beer. None of us were anywhere near the legal drinking age in Maryland (21), but we thought we could be discreet.

That was my first mistake.

When we showed up in Ocean City, we were able to get all of us into a shabby motel down at the bottom of the beach. The beer drinking began immediately. At the time, and for quite a while thereafter, I was known as "One-Drink Barrow." I was extremely sensitive to alcohol and became inebriated after only one or two beers.

On this occasion, we had cases and cases of beer, and I was soon way past my limit.

That was my second mistake.

Unfortunately for me, most of my classmates were pretty far gone as well. All but one, Henry Hopkins. At that time Henry did not drink, but he still liked to hang out with his drunken classmates, for some ungodly reason that I will never understand.

One of my classmates, Otts Davis, was almost as drunk as I was. Suddenly, out of nowhere, he had a vision that the cops were on to us and were pulling into the motel parking lot. This was not true, but he came running in, scared witless, screaming "the cops are coming—hide the beer."

There was no hiding the beer—empty cans were everywhere. It was hopeless. So instead, we fled the scene. I ran out the door and headed for the ocean. Thinking clearly, I reasoned: "They will never catch me out in the ocean. I can swim away." The beach was right out front and there was a long stone jetty that stuck out into the Atlantic Ocean. I ran down the jetty at top speed and dove into what I thought was the ocean.

That was my third mistake.

Unfortunately, the tide had gone out and the ocean was no longer there. Instead there was only a hard bottom of rocks, oyster shells, and broken glass. I had a bad landing and cut myself to pieces. I hardly felt a thing, however.

When I returned to the motel room, the others yelled at me that I was messing the place up by bleeding all over everything. So they pushed me into the bathroom and told me to get in the bathtub. Someone turned on the water. I fell asleep as the tub filled with water and blood.

At some point, my friend Henry showed up and asked, "Where's Barrow?" The other drunkards pointed to the bathroom. Henry came in, took one look, and said, "We gotta get this guy to the emergency room, now!" My classmates were unconcerned. It was Henry alone who cleaned me up, put a towel around my arm to stem the bleeding from multiple gashes, stashed me in the back of his car, and drove me to the fire station down the road. But no one was there. After looking in the yellow pages at a public phone both, he drove to a doctor's office nearby. Fortunately, the doc's office was in his home.

After the doctor sewed me up and made a few wisecracks about drunken kids at the beach, he sent Henry and me on our way in the early morning hours.

I survived that whole series of reckless decisions only because one well-intentioned, sober person just happened to come by the right place at the right time.

Note to Henry: Thank you, Henry. You saved my life. It also appears that I may owe you for one doctor's bill, plus interest for more than 60 years. Send me the bill.

3

CARS AND MOTORCYCLES

MOTORCYCLES I HAVE LOVED (AND LOST)

Find what you love and let it kill you.
              –attributed to Kinky Friedman

I woke up on the icy street. The sleeves of my cool black leather motorcycle jacket were shredded. I had bloody abrasions all over. As consciousness slowly returned, I saw a flashing red "EMERGENCY ROOM" sign just a few yards away. I thought to myself, "Well. This is it. I have finally killed myself on that damn motorcycle."

How did I get there? Because, as my brother says, I'm a numbskull.

In a family Zoom meeting recently, my younger brother, Jake, suggested that I compile all of my memoirs into a book and call it "Adventures of a Lucky Numbskull." He thought it would sell well on Amazon Books.

I did compile these memoirs. But I didn't think that title would sell. Besides, the "numbskull" part did not appeal to me. I do admit, however, that Jake's suggestion epitomizes many of the experiences of my childhood, adolescence, and early life.

It occurred to me in talking to Jake that some of the most stupid things I have done arose out of my love of motorcycles. I always felt called to ride things recklessly. Horses. Bicycles. Any vehicle. My motorcycles answered that call completely.

I started buying bikes shortly after I got my driver's license. Motorcycles are built to do stupid and reckless things. The fact that I am still alive writing this book at age 80 is amazing to me and to everyone who knew me when I was in my motorcycle phase.

Motorcycles have always had an almost religious, masculine mystique about them. Think of the films—*The Wild One*, *Easy Rider*, and *Rebel Without a Cause*—and the famed book, *Zen and the Art of Motorcycle Maintenance*. In another book, a famed Harley Davidson ethnography, the authors identify four factors contributing to the spirituality of motorcycle riding: "the closeness to nature, the heightened sensory awareness, the mantric throbbing of the engine, the constant awareness of risk and the…mental focus."[7] That's a fancy way of saying that riding a motorcycle is nothing like driving a car. On a bike, you see, feel, and smell everything around you in a uniquely direct way. You also feel connected to your ride in an intimate way that no ride in a car can compare to. It can be a beautiful experience. If you survive it.

It is always a mistake to ride a motorcycle fast. You are a few pounds of bone and vulnerable protoplasm going 75 or 80 miles an hour, more or less, in the midst of hundreds of cars and large trucks, most of the drivers of which do not even see you, and some of which are driven by hostile rednecks who would just as soon run you off the road as look at you. (Remember, that is how Peter Fonda met his end in the classic biker film, *Easy Rider*.)

Oddly enough, the riskiness never entered my mind. Riding a motorcycle made me feel immortal and invulnerable. Nothing, of course, could be further from the truth. I was blinded by the romance of riding fast and saw only how exquisite the experience was. The rational part of a man's brain, at least my brain, completely shuts off

---

[7] John W. Schouten and James H. McAlexander, "Subcultures of Consumption: An Ethnography of the New Bikers," *Journal of Consumer Research* 22, no. 1 (June 1995): 43-61.

in the presence of a beautiful shiny piece of motorcycle metal. When the engine starts to throb, adulation turns into true love.

It is not uncommon for people to have a blind spot about the extreme danger of motorbikes. In his book *On the Move*, the famed writer, psychologist, and neurologist Oliver Sacks reveals that he was a motorcycle nut. He suffered wrecks and injuries from that passion (as well as other risky endeavors). Despite his exhaustive knowledge of psychology and neurology and his excellent self-awareness, he says he was completely oblivious to the dangers involved in riding motorcycles way too fast. A gigantic blind spot existed in the brain of a famous world-class brain scientist. I shared that same blind spot.

My first motorbike was a BMW R27, a single-lung beauty that looked like it should have been ridden by a German officer in WWII. Unlike most motorcycles, it was quiet, with a smooth ride. No loud exhaust noise belched from the tailpipes to annoy bystanders and ruin the peaceful rides I loved to take through country roads.

I favored European bikes. I always hated the high-pitched scream of a Japanese "crotch rocket." No whiny Asian machines or gigantic, overweight, bolt-on Harleys for me. Harleys were the noisiest of all. They also symbolized to me American excess and obesity. Not my thing. My favorites were, and still are, the British, German, and Italian bikes, especially the quiet, smooth-riding, and beautifully engineered BMWs.

A BMW R27

I rode my beautiful BMW everywhere in college and law school and at my summer job in Vermont. I covered hundreds of rural roads among the magnificent hills, valleys, and mountains of the state of Vermont. Vermont was made to order for rural scenic riding. It offered a high better than any from drugs.

Every year while I was in law school, I rode nonstop 920 miles from Cambridge, Massachusetts, to Asheville, North Carolina, and back—a trip that always ended with the entire front of my face and body covered in a thick coat of insects. The bike did not have a windshield. That would have ruined its classic looks.

I first wrecked my beloved BMW on a drunken ride up Howland Road where my dad lived, on Sunset Mountain in Asheville. My draft board physical was only a week away, but I did so much damage to myself in that mishap that the military labeled me 4F.

I still suffer from the various bone injuries I acquired in that besotted episode. I flew off the bike and wound up in a tree halfway down the mountain. I had been quaffing more than a few "sodas" at the Brown Derby Bar just outside of town. The alcohol did not enhance my driving skills. I paid dearly for that mistake: I still limp on one leg. But at least I avoided a round trip to Vietnam, returning in a body bag.

The BMW survived the Sunset Mountain wreck better than I did. After the accident, I drove it back to law school. But there it finally met its end. On my way to class from my cozy abode in the slums of Lechmere during a blinding snow storm, an old lady failed to see me speeding to the Harvard campus. She pulled out in front of me from a side street. I crashed into her car, crumpling the bike. I went flying over the hood and onto the sidewalk, landing flat on my back, in front of the Cambridge City hospital. Instead of being driven to the emergency room, I had managed to crash-land in front of it.

I realized I was not in bad shape, apart from some abrasions, however. I parked the bike and walked to class.

After the BMW went to the junkyard, I fell head over heels for a Triumph Bonneville 650. Another questionable love affair.

A Triumph Bonneville

That Triumph was slick; a sexy-looking hunk of metal. It had the kind of acceleration that could nearly break your neck when you put the hammer down. It was about the coolest thing on wheels I had ever seen (except maybe for its cousins, the other British classics, the BSA and the Norton.) It was so much fun to ride I could hardly believe it.

Triumph bikes had a great pedigree. They gained popularity in the U.S. when Marlon Brando rode a 1950 Thunderbird 6T in the 1953 film *The Wild One*. Then, in 1969, a Bonneville won the insane Isle of Man race going an average of 99.99 miles per hour. For Triumph fans, the 1969 Bonneville was the best Triumph ever.

The legend lives on. Bruce Springsteen was riding a Triumph in New Jersey in February of 2021 when he was busted by the National Park Police for driving under the influence of tequila.

Triumphs were so popular they were copied by Harley-Davidson for their "small" bike, the Sportster. But with its anachronistic V-twin, the Sportster was no match for the Bonneville.

The major problem with the Bonneville was that on slippery turns, especially with wet leaves on the road, the rear wheel would slide sideways across the road into the dirt. I would jerk my lower leg out of harm's way and try to stay on top of the upper side of the fast-moving hunk of metal sliding on its side into God knows what. That happened several times. Those events gave new meaning to the phrase "closeness to nature," as I scraped leaves and mud off my body. The only injuries I had from those put-downs were a lot of burns on my leg where it was pressed into the hot exhaust pipe. Still have those scars.

At speeds above 90 mph, the Triumph had some odd vibrations. Occasionally, bolts would come loose. British engineering. It was not uncommon to have various parts vibrate enough to fall off the bike during a long high-speed run. Fortunately, it was usually only the kickstand that disappeared.

I sold the Triumph before it killed me. I bought other bikes over the years, but nothing ever as intoxicating as that Bonneville. Japanese Hondas and Suzukis drove the Triumph company out of business. Now it's back, and making nice bikes again. The old ones, like mine, are vintage treasures, selling for nearly $20,000 on eBay.

Even to this day, I have a thing for a good-looking bike. If I see something like a Moto Guzzi parked on the street, I have to pause and drool.

Maybe I need to get myself one of those pretty things and hit the road again before I turn 90. Wouldn't that be fun?! (Although it could also turn out to be a mistake . . .)

How To Destroy A Perfectly Good Car

I like to race sailboats, even though I am well past my shelf life as a competitive sailor at age 80. Sailboats are not as fast as motorcycles or cars, but in the races there can be a lot of boats crowding together, trying to cross a start line first or get around a mark of the course in front of another boat. Collisions are not uncommon. There can be a lot of near misses, screaming and yelling, and legal protests taken to boat court. It's not unusual to hear the familiar crunch of fiberglass breaking as one boat crashes at full speed into the hull of another.

I love it all.

Skittering past another boat and driving her off course, or passing another racer at close quarters, is part of the fun of sailboat racing. Gets my adrenaline going. Drives my fun meter up into the red zone. When my brother Henry is aboard, he hates this part. I am on the tiller driving the boat, and he is up forward watching the near misses. It brings back bad memories, he says.

The hard fact is: Henry has never trusted my driving, whether it be a boat, car, or motorcycle. There is a valid reason for that. It has to do with my driving technique when I was 16 and he was 14, forced to sit in the suicide seat while I imagined myself to be on a race course going as fast as possible, especially downhill and around curves. He never liked that.

My first car, acquired at age 16, was a green 1949 Studebaker sedan. I got it from Frank Thomas, a friend of my parents. It had been sitting in his driveway taking up space for a few years. He said I could have it if I could get it off his property. The battery was dead as a doornail. I had no idea if there was anything else wrong with it. Taking the leap (as I was always predisposed to do in my teenage years), I pushed it out of his driveway in Ruxton, Maryland, and over to the top of a small hill nearby. I got in with high hopes and headed down the hill in neutral with my foot pumping the accelerator. Just as I neared the bottom, I popped the clutch into first gear. Lo and behold, it coughed and started up. I drove it home right then, before Mr. Thomas could change his mind.

I had the Studebaker for several years without any problems. It took me everywhere. When my parents split up and my dad moved from the farm in Maryland to Asheville, I drove it down there and back to Maryland several times. It was a great old car. Down in Asheville where my dad had moved, his house was situated on the upper part of Sunset Mountain. Howland Road ran by the front of the house and down the hill to Sunset Boulevard. It was a steep and winding hill. The most fun thing to do on that road was to scream downhill at top speed in the Studebaker and see if I could get it up on two wheels on the curves. I did that successfully many times. When Henry was in the car with me, he would climb into the back seat as soon as he realized what I was up to. He would hide on the floor in the back, screaming at me to stop and threatening to rat me out to our dad. His yelling at me, for some peculiar reason, gave the whole experience an extra zing. (Later, of course, I tackled the same road on motorcycles.)

The Studebaker was a classic with a reliable flathead 6 engine. Unfortunately, it was not designed for the speeds I preferred to drive—80-90 mph. On its final trip, a run from Asheville back to Maryland, I made a big mistake. I gunned it up over 90 and the engine blew up. Threw a piston rod right through the block. It was curtains for that car.

My brother Henry was with me, and he was pissed. We were stuck in a little crossroads on Route 1 called Dinwiddie, Virginia, south of Richmond, more than 100 miles from home. We called our mother and she said she would come get us. We stayed in a fleabag motel for a day or so eating peanut butter sandwiches until she showed up. The Studebaker was towed to the junk yard.[8]

I still miss that car.

---

[8] Henry offered these comments on this story: "It wasn't just the peanut butter sandwiches you made me eat after the breakdown that pissed me off. It was also the fact that you insisted that we ignore the two young girls, just our age, who were the daughters of the motel owner. That was where you made your worst mistake. Missed opportunity for both of us."

Even my other brother, Jake, had something to say about the demise of the Studebaker: "I remember this one too. I liked those opposing doors. I was told that you didn't ever once put oil into the engine and didn't know you had to do that, so it ran dry and threw the rod. I'm sure speed contributed, but I think it was mainly the oil."

A wrecked VW bug

I now have a new car, at least new to me. It's a bright red Volkswagen (VW) beetle. My brother Jake has advice for me about this car, since he has driven a number of VW bugs over the years and flipped no less than three of them right over on their tops. I hereby quote his advice without editorial comment; you can draw your own conclusions about its merits:

> "Warning! Don't take any curves in a VW bug over the speed limit when the road cants away from the curve direction. The wheels will buckle and you go over. Another important rule for driving those things is—stay off the booze."—Jake Barrow

4

COLLEGE AND LAW SCHOOL

REBEL WITHOUT A CAUSE

Joe was in the class ahead of me in college. He was many years ahead of me in terms of inventive anarchist inclinations. I think he was from Texas or around those parts. Joe was a genuine rebel. He was the James Dean of Yale. Even the way he wore his clothes—no preppy stuff from J. Press, just filthy raggedy jeans—was, to me anyway, the sign of a new leader. I was enamored by his style. I became his sidekick.

I am not sure why Joe was such a rebellious iconoclast, always poking at the system. It may have been the same reason that affected me. I was on a weighty scholarship, which should have made me a grateful and obedient serf. Yale had a system for making sure that scholarship students knew their place. You had to work every day if you were on a scholarship. That would not have been bad if some of the jobs had not been humiliating and degrading. It was fine to work in the back of the kitchen or library, but first you had to wear a white apron and wait on your classmates in the dining rooms, cleaning up their slop. This situation gave rise to some cognitive dissonance on the part of scholarship students: a mix of resentment and appreciation leading to frustration and anti-authoritarian behavior. Occasionally the snotty behavior of my classmates required that a tray of slop be accidentally dropped in their fancy-pants laps by scholarship peons like me.

Joe's behavior was comparable. He made a mess of the Pierson College lawn—playing Frisbee and football on the carefully manicured grass, turning it into a mud hole. Despite pleas from the college dean, it became a scandalous disgrace. It was so bad that students from other colleges began to refer to our lawn as the "Pierson Pig Pen." I felt some perverse pride in that, but not everyone agreed.

Joe also broke the dress code at Yale. At least, he pushed it over the edge. The dress code had already been reduced to the bare minimum: by 1963 it required only wearing a coat and tie at meals, instead of wearing a coat and tie all day, which had been required for the past 200 years or so.

Joe decided to destroy the dress code completely. His strategy was to follow it literally. He began by wearing a filthy tie and raggedy coat but no collared shirt. This caused consternation among the deans and other authorities, but they could not argue that he was not in compliance. They made no move against him. So he persisted and people soon followed, especially me. I was right there with him in the dining room, with coat and tie but no shirt.

Pretty soon everyone got used to it, and it became no big deal. Wear a shirt if you felt like it. Or not.

So, of course, Joe decided that everyone had adjusted too smoothly to the "shirtless" thing, and he decided to go pantless as well. He took to the dining room with only coat, tie, and underwear. I could never bring myself to go that far, no matter how much I admired Joe.

Joe's undergraduate revolution continued to reverberate for years at the stuffy Yale Club in New York. According to a 2015 article, "The Yale Club . . . is descending into chaos" as more and more students rebel against its strict standards of dress.[9] I've heard that the dress-code anarchy continues today. Who knows what it will lead to?

I was lucky that, for me, it led to no serious consequences beyond

---

[9] Rachel Tashjian, "The Yale Club Is Not Upholding Its Dress Code and Is Descending into Chaos," *Vanity Fair*, June 17, 2015.

being urged by the dean to keep my pants on. It didn't end up on my transcript.

I lost track of Joe after college. I heard he was a very successful builder of homes for low-income people. If so, I am still a fan.

KING OF THE MOON

I was on the street behind Yale's Pierson College late at night. I was with a few other miscreants who enjoyed the same kind of stupid pranks as I did. Our pants and underwear were down around our ankles. We were bent over looking backwards through our legs at a busload of girls from Smith College.

Of all the idiotic and (in hindsight) embarrassing pranks I ever got up to, this one takes the cake.

The girls were screaming and yelling and throwing stuff at us out of the bus windows. I imagined that the stuff thrown our way was mostly love notes with the girls' phone numbers or other signs of affection. Later I was dismayed to discover that it was mostly used tampons, empty soda cans, and other trash.

Suddenly, I caught sight of the campus police heading our way. We all pulled up our pants and ran like hell in the opposite direction of the cops. We always made a clean getaway.

Back in the 1960s when I was in college, there were strange cultural customs in vogue among young males. One was called "mooning." You performed a "moon" by "dropping trou," bending over, looking through your legs, and aiming your bare butt at the intended beneficiaries, usually a group of young women.

Often the mooning was done from a car so that one could press one's hairy butt up against a window or just hang it outside the window as the girls passed by. This was particularly satisfying.

For some bewildering reason, mooning was a popular practice in the 1960s. It was considered a sign of male admiration for the ladies. Or perhaps lust. Who knows? In any case, it was regarded by the performers as an act of high praise to the recipients, and in return, we thought the ladies would be favorably impressed. The recipients usually responded with shouts and throwing items, although sometimes they added hostile remarks, such as: "Put your pants on, jerk! You make me throw up!" This was confusing to us mooners.

Living in an all-male institution and being occasionally visited by a large group of females from an all-female institution can lead to delusional thinking and peculiar behavior. We had no idea how to properly impress the ladies, and they likewise must have been totally baffled by our ridiculous and, frankly, disgusting antics.

I had no sisters growing up, and I went to an all-male high school before college at Yale, which was then all male also. I had no clue about women, what they wanted, what they liked, how to attract them. I was totally befuddled by these creatures, even though I was very strongly attracted to them. In some demented way I thought that mooning them would get me favorable attention.

The leader of the pack at my college, as far as mooning and many other interesting and inventive games were concerned, was the same Joe who starred in the previous story. Joe was a leader in all things humorous, fun, and rebellious. Mooning was made to order for Joe and distinctly frowned upon by the authorities and by the stuffier students. In fact, it was probably a violation of some kind of law.

I was vulnerable to Joe's charisma. He easily brought me into the practice of mooning, as an apprentice, of course.

Some of my fondest college memories are of the times that Joe and I and other co-conspirators took our stand, lined up in our favorite location on Church Street where the buses from various all-girls colleges (like Vassar, Smith, Mt. Holyoke, and Wellesley) parked after bringing the young ladies to New Haven for events euphemistically called "mixers."

The only thing that ever got mixed at mixers was a lot of grain alcohol. The male participants at a "mixer" were mostly just mixed up by the whole event and confused about what the hell was going on. Were these girls being brought in to get laid, or drunk, or what?

In any case, the ladies were unfortunately required to go home after the mixer to their respective schools, whether they got drunk or laid or not. They dutifully trooped out to buses at the back of the college and boarded up. That's when Joe, together with his team of mooners, hit the sidewalk, pants and underwear down around their ankles and their hairy butts pointed at the buses.

The girls always went nuts, cheering (or maybe it was jeering?), throwing out their underwear, bras, trash, and various other things, yelling insults or claiming that they were in love. It was confusing. Insane. Just participating in these ridiculous events was one of the highlights of my college career. The most thrilling part was when the young ladies took up the game themselves, mooning us from the bus windows.

There are few more exciting sights than a busload of beautiful college girls with their rear ends pressed firmly against the glass of bus windows. Exquisite.

Unfortunately, somewhere along the line we began to realize that our performances were not having the intended effect. The first hint was when we realized that none of us had gotten any dates or phone numbers or love letters or, in fact, any positive response of any kind whatsoever from the young ladies we were working so hard to impress. This was disappointing. Sad and depressing, actually.

What was wrong with these women? Did they not realize that mooning was more than just an expression of our admiration? It was an art form as well.[10] Even Michelangelo painted a magnificent picture of God mooning the universe as he created heaven and earth. The painting is in the Sistine Chapel.

---

[10] Mooning has an ancient pedigree, going all the way back to Roman times, according to "Mooning," a page on Wikipedia, accessed December 30, 2022, https://en.wikipedia.org/wiki/Mooning. It died out as a college prank after the 1960s, but more recently (1995), students at Stanford University (a very serious place) conducted a "mass mooning" in protest of censorship. In January 2006, a Maryland state circuit court legitimized the act by holding that mooning is a form of artistic expression protected by the First Amendment.

Michelangelo's painting of God mooning the world

Our best efforts to attract the opposite sex had come to naught. We were going to have to come up with a new and different strategy. As a result, mooning eventually faded away at Yale. To me, this was a cultural loss, but I suspect others may feel differently about it.[11]

Later in life I had an experience that demonstrated to me how much times have changed, and for the better. I was sailing peacefully, alone, down a waterway in Florida in my cruising sailboat when a powerboat pulled up next to me from behind. Inside the boat was one young guy and about seven stunningly perfect college-age girls in bikinis. There was a large keg in the middle of the boat with several

---

[11] I forwarded an earlier draft of this story to one of my roommates from college, Dave Mills, for fact-checking purposes. He wrote me back the following: "You left out the part about you mooning my wife-to-be (now my wife, Sherry) when she came to visit every Friday night. I vividly remember that she regarded it a token of your great affection for her." So true. I admired Sherry so much that I was willing to give her the ultimate greeting. I still love her, but I no longer greet her with exactly the same end. After all, she is now a married woman with two grown sons.

hoses from which to quaff beer. As the powerboat slowed down, the guy driving grinned broadly at me and then said something to the girls. I looked over in amazement as all the girls removed their bikini tops, faced me, and began waving at me. I was so stunned that I almost drove the boat aground.

Mooning has definitely evolved into nicer and better things.

ABANDONED AT VASSAR

The sun came up. I was under the snow near some kind of gate. I was not particularly cold, but I was miserably hung over. I dug out and looked around. "How did I end up here? I must have blacked out," I thought.

Then, the realization began to dawn on me. I was near the entrance to Vassar College. It was Sunday after a long night of ferocious partying. But where was my ride back to Yale? "Where's Froggie? How the hell am I going to get to New Haven?" I pondered.

When I was in college, an all-male school in Connecticut, one of the all-girls colleges was only an hour or so drive away—Vassar. All day, every day, all week long, we dreamed of Vassar girls. I have no idea what they were dreaming of, but based on how we were received when we showed up there, I think they were thinking pretty much the same way we were.

Every weekend, the call was "ROAD TRIP!" Usually 75 miles to Vassar. Sometimes to Smith or Mt. Holyoke or maybe even farther afield.

Believe me, these trips were adventures. The dangerous part was the alcohol consumption involved in the drive up to Poughkeepsie, New York, and then . . . even more daunting . . . the drive back.

This particular weekend, I had hit the Vassar mixers with a guy who roomed near me, known as Froggie. Froggie was a fun guy to hang with but not much of a chick magnet because, even though he had buckets of money as an heir to the DuPont family fortune in Delaware, he was short and plump. He had been given the names

"Frog" and "Froggie" at Hotchkiss (his prep school) because, when wearing his glasses, he had a slightly frog-like resemblance.

High-school boys can be bullies—cruel and insulting to everyone when they can get away with it. Degrading nicknames are only the beginning. Froggie's unfortunate name did not bother me a bit, however. I liked Froggie. Plus, he had a good ride, a brand new Aston Martin convertible.

So off I went to Vassar with Froggie in the Aston Martin. He had recently bought the car from a dealer in Manhattan and did not have a clue how to drive it. He always drove it way too fast.

Of course, I have little memory of what went on that night. The alcohol intake took care of any memory issues. I heard later that some classmates from my high school in Baltimore were there from Princeton that same night, for a big Vassar extravaganza. I am not sure whether I saw them or not. Forty years later, they told me that they met me there, and that I was on a drunken rampage.

Could be true, but they often exaggerate.

I fell asleep in the snowbank while waiting for Froggie to drive me home. When it got really cold, I burrowed deeper into the snow and dozed away in an alcoholic slumber.

When the sun came up, I dug out and looked around. I was in a predicament: no ride back to school and struggling with a horrible hangover.

I don't remember how I solved that problem, but I am grateful that I was not in the Aston Martin on the return to New Haven. Froggie crashed into a toll booth on the Merritt Parkway.

He survived but the car did not.

That was not Froggie's only bad trip. My roommate, Bob Dunlop, wrote to me recently: "I recall the Aston Martin well. Froggie crashed it into another group of Yale guys on the way to Vassar. I was sitting in the front seat and miraculously had a seat belt on, but still my face landed on the windshield. I ended up in the Emergency Room in Poughkeepsie with a broken nose."

THE GREAT GATSBY

Recently, I read an article in *The New Yorker* about the origins of today's take-no-prisoners, scorched-earth Republican Party.[12] The author mentions how it all got started in Greenwich, Connecticut, at the home of an extremely wealthy couple, Lee Hanley and his wife Allie.

Suddenly I realized: "I knew that guy!"

According to the article, "In a Georgian manor overlooking a lake [in Greenwich], lived Lee and Allie Hanley, who were early converts to the radical conservative movement. Lee had graduated from St. Paul's and from Yale, where he played polo, squash, and soccer. . . . He was a bon vivant, with a fondness for salmon-colored slacks, and a ready checkbook for political ventures. 'Very warm and engaging,' a Greenwich friend said. 'A collector of curiosities, a Renaissance man at sort of a superficial level.'"

I realized that I was one of the "curiosities" that Lee had collected.

Lee and Allie were not the kind of people I typically hung out with back in my college days. We met in other circumstances.

I had gone on an outstandingly debauched spring break from college—a disgraceful, drunken, womanizing spree in Nassau. By the time it was over, I was a stinking, filthy, hung-over mess and had lost all my money. I had only one thing left, a return airline ticket to Palm Beach, Florida. When I got off the plane at the Palm Beach airport, I called my Uncle Arthur—collect, of course. Uncle Arthur lived in West Palm Beach. I begged him to bail me out.

Uncle Arthur had four children of his own, three daughters and one son, so he was no novice when it came to misbehaving kids. He read me the Riot Act, but came to the airport anyway, picked me up and took me to his house. There I got a shower and some food. I tried to pay my way by teaching one of his daughters how to dance to Chubby Checker with a hula hoop. I am not sure how much that was

---

[12] Evan Osnos, "How Greenwich Republicans Learned to Love Trump," *The New Yorker*, May 3, 2020.

appreciated by Uncle Arthur. Not much, I think. He decided to get rid of me as soon as possible to avoid any additional influence I might have on his daughters.

My dear uncle gave me $5 and took me out to the highway north from Palm Beach. "Good luck getting to Connecticut," he said. I needed to get back to New Haven in time for the start of classes. Hitchhiking was my only means of making that happen. In the 1960s, it was still possible.

I put on my Yale jacket and stuck my thumb out, hoping for a ride to somewhere at least a little north of Palm Beach.

Within five minutes a car stopped. It was a brand-new, beautiful, silver Rolls Royce. Inside was a young couple leaving their mansion in Palm Beach, headed north to another mansion in Connecticut! What incredible luck! The driver was Lee Hanley, a student at Yale at the time. He was in one of my classes, but I had not met him before this incident. He said, "I could use some help driving. Do you have a license?"

"Of course I have a license, but I have zero dollars. I got robbed in the Bahamas," I lied to him. Lee responded, "I will loan you some money for food, and we will also stop in a motel for a night. I will loan you some money for that too."

I could not believe my luck—though I have to admit, things like that seemed to happen to me all the time. Somebody stepped into my disaster and pulled me to safety. Invariably, as a young boy, a teenager, and a college kid, I found myself in a bad fix due to something incredibly careless and stupid that I did. Then, out of nowhere, a Good Samaritan saved my bacon. Now it was happening again.

Lee and his wife, Allie—who was stunningly beautiful—and I had a nice trip in the Rolls all the way to New Haven. Lee and Allie lived off campus in a huge mansion with about 10 acres of lawn and a bunch of polo ponies. He was on the Yale polo team, of course.

During the two-day drive north, we enjoyed talking about the classes we had taken, a crazy French literature professor we knew who used to run around the streets of New Haven naked as a jaybird late at night, and all the other wonderful aspects of undergraduate life at Yale in the 1960s.

At one point during the trip, I realized that I was like a character in a 1960s version of F. Scott Fitzgerald's story, *The Great Gatsby*. Lee WAS Gatsby, and I was Nick! Except that unlike the imposter Gatsby, Lee was the real deal, the wealthy upper class WASP, with the right looks, the right accent, the right car, the right wife, the right prep school, the right college, and all the other features that Fitzgerald's Gatsby would have killed for.

I did manage to pay Lee back for the loan, but I was not moving in his elite circles at college, so I never saw much of him again, other than a passing "hello" on the way to or from classes.

I was amazed to learn, 50 years later, that Lee—a generous and nice guy, I thought—had used some of his vast fortune to give birth to today's cruel and racist Make America Great Again (MAGA) movement. Maybe I did not know Lee as well as I thought.

My cousin Laura remembers her father, my Uncle Arthur, bailing me out and sending me on my way back to Yale. She says, however: "I'm pretty sure you taught me the Twist to the Beatles' 'Twist & Shout,' not Chubby Checker's, and Daddy wouldn't be so cheap as to give you only $5; I think it was $20."

All I can say is: no human memory is perfect.

WHAT'S NEXT?

After law school, what should I do? This was a real dilemma. I had absolutely no interest in practicing law, fighting over someone else's problems in a court or conference room.

I had escaped the war by engaging in risky activities involving alcohol and a motorcycle, totally destroying my right ankle. I was drafted and showed up on crutches at my physical. After reviewing my X-rays, the Army doctor reluctantly gave me a pass. So death in the Vietnam jungle was not in my future.

With good grades from Harvard Law, you have a ticket to Wall

Street law firms or any other top-of-the-line law firms worldwide. (I interviewed with a Tokyo firm for a summer job one year.) You can clerk for a judge. Or you can go into teaching at one of the lesser law schools if you were on law review.

If you are the typical aggressive/combative Harvard student, you can become a prosecutor for a few years, beating the crap out of overworked public defenders in court. Then you can join the high-paid defense bar where you get to defend celebrities, famous polluters, billionaire plunderers, and scammers like Bernie Madoff, or famous sexual predators like Harvey Weinstein and Jeffrey Epstein, earning truckloads of money.

Some years after law school I came across the non-fiction book and movie *A Civil Action*, in which pollution by chemical companies had poisoned many families in the Boston area, killing numerous children. The families were represented by an ambulance-chasing lawyer, who was up against powerful Boston law firms with deep pockets and stacked deep with Harvard grads.

One of the attorneys defending the chemical companies was a former classmate of mine at Harvard Law School. He made sure that the parents of the dead children got nothing. After reading this nauseating book, I called him up at his posh Boston law firm to ask him how he felt about being portrayed in the book as an arch-villain and child-killing monster. He laughed and said he was pretty proud of the victory he had won on behalf of the polluters. "It was good for business," he said.

Another option is politics. Some Harvard Law grads stand on the battle lines of cultural wars, attacking women, gays, transgender people, black people, poor people, and liberals of various kinds from positions of power in government.

Even for those lawyers who disposed of their ethical sensitivities by their second year in law school, there are downsides to the elite jobs that Harvard grads migrate to. The big firms will work you to death, up to 13 hours a day, six or seven days a week—while the partners are out on the golf course or getting plastered at exclusive clubs, attracting new high-paying corporate clients. It's how the law-firm business plan works.

The salaries are astronomical, but the pressure can destroy your health. I met a young lady in 2020 who was working for a big D.C. law firm. Six months into the job, she had a stress-induced stroke and will probably never work again.

Is it worth it? I didn't think so.

I never belonged in law school in the first place, and didn't want to ruin any more of my life. Instead of a large law firm, I took a low-paying, low-visibility job in the government. The job involved no legal combat, just doing legal writing for members of Congressional committees. It was a job of enviable anonymity, in which you pretended that everything you wrote was actually written by someone else—a politician. Unlike law firms, vacations in my office could stretch for weeks or even months, depending on Congressional elections and recess schedules.

That worked out well for me. I passed up the country club membership, the new Mercedes, and the mansion in the gated community, but I did a lot of kayaking, partying, traveling, and sailing, and, until later in life, never worked on weekends.

5

AN IRRESPONSIBLE YOUNG ADULT

PARTY GAMES

The secret to a happy life is to pursue meaningless goals.
—unknown

In my deranged youth, I was a fan of party games. These usually developed in bars or campsites where rednecks congregated. The first I came across was the game of Cornhole. When I first heard that people were playing Cornhole, I was terrified. I thought: "That is not a game, man! That is serious sexual abuse." A friend asked me to go play Cornhole with him and I said to him: "You better step back and shut up!"

As it turned out, however, the name of the game had nothing to do with the actual game, which involved throwing little sacks of dried corn into a hole in a board. Whew! What a relief! The game even became a family affair, played in backyards. It was soon taken over by corporate interests who realized that they could make a buck selling the boards and bags. The amazing thing to me was that they never changed the name to something less X-rated. I played a few times but it never got me going. Not like the game of Butt Darts did.

Butt Darts was my kind of game, a truly competitive game of skill. And money could be made betting on the results.

Butt Darts originated in the backwoods of eastern Kentucky, where there was not a lot of recreational activity other than hunting and fishing. It was a *Deliverance* kind of place. Butt Darts is the classic redneck game, a game that you play when the hunting is bad and you and your buddies are bored to death around a campfire in the woods.

There was a famous river in the woods of eastern Kentucky—the Russell Fork—which was a seasonal Mecca for whitewater kayakers from all over the east coast. The hunting areas around the Russell Fork were like a virus hot spot for Butt Darts among the local boys.

Whitewater kayakers running the Russell Fork with local boaters quickly picked up the Butt Darts game and brought it back to urban areas like Washington, D.C., where it became an instant fad at parties and festivals attended by kayakers. I loved the game and practiced often in hopes of winning bets.

Butt Darts involves inserting a quarter in your rear end, between the butt cheeks, and holding it in place, fully clothed. I emphasize FULLY CLOTHED because people always get that wrong. A shot glass is placed between your legs on the floor. You win the game, and usually a few bets, if you can drop the quarter into the shot glass. Not as easy as it sounds. I won a lot of money at Butt Darts because I practiced at home to keep my skills at the top level.

Although the game was a hit with young kayakers, it had limited appeal elsewhere. Later in life, I occasionally tried to introduce it at parties. Not only did people look at me askance and walk the other way, but some of the women never spoke to me again.

Why is the game of Butt Darts included in this book, you might ask. Basically because it is a disgraceful waste of time. A worthless skill that serves no meaningful purpose. I have learned from this, however, and someday—soon, maybe—I may stop trying to learn totally worthless skills which have no socially redeeming value and which can only lead to embarrassment and disgrace.

Not very likely, though.

THE VIEW FROM THE TREE

My first job as a young lawyer in Washington, D.C., was in an obscure and rather austere office filled with serious, mostly elderly, lawyers. Oddly, I was comfortable in that job, with its rigid rules of behavior. It was like an anchor to reality because—in my life outside the office—many of my friends were living an alternative lifestyle, in communes and group houses, with no jobs or ties to the "establishment." Smoking joints and taking drugs were part of their normal, everyday life.

There were definitely no potheads or people with an alternative lifestyle in my office. It was a buttoned-up place with a rigorous dress code. A young lawyer would be sent home immediately if he was seen in or around the office without a coat and tie. I was once reprimanded for not having a tie when I actually had one on, but it was covered up by the neck of my sweater. I never let on to my office mates that I had smoked pot. That kind of behavior would have been shocking to everyone in the office—and it would have been curtains for my employment there.

One of my mentors, Robert, was a fellow Yale graduate. I liked him and looked up to him. However, he was about as far from a rebellious miscreant as one could be. He was brilliant and serious, but also funny and generous. He was 100% straight as far as recreational drugs were concerned, like everyone else in that office, but I never held that against him.

Robert and I were getting to be fairly good friends, but one incident solidified my respect for him forever. The critical incident occurred the morning after my younger brother Henry came to visit me in my apartment above a dry cleaning store on East Capitol Street.

Henry has to this day never participated in the normal commercial world. He has an independent streak and has never had an employer, choosing to work on his own as an artist, farmer, and woodworker. When he came to visit me, he was living the epitome of the alternative lifestyle.

Henry suggested that I try some "really good stuff" he had

acquired from a friend in California. "Go ahead, Pope. You will love it. It will clear things up for you in a new way. Come on, Pope. Don't be a chicken." I was not too sure I could trust Henry on this.

But . . . then he said the magic words. "You will have a hell of a lot of fun!"

I swallowed the pill.

The stuff went down easy and produced a very unusual and interesting experience. It was amazing fun. Henry had not lied about that, at least. But it was also disorienting and long lasting.

The next morning, I was still flying high and enjoying an incredibly beautiful, out-of-this world experience. I was happy and carefree. Suddenly, a troubling thought came to mind. It was Wednesday morning. I was scheduled to be at work.

I said to Henry, "I am supposed to be at work today. What should I do?" Henry, thinking only of my welfare, of course, advised me: "Go on in to the office. It will be even more fun. You will have a great time."

Trusting his words, and ignoring the strange smirk on his face, I eagerly bounced out the door and sauntered happily down the street toward my office, a few blocks away. Everything—the trees, the flowers, the buildings—looked exquisitely beautiful and new in the sparkling sunshine. It was the most beautiful walk to work I had ever experienced.

I was happily skipping along East Capitol Street towards the Capitol when I noticed some of the people on the sidewalk looking at me kind of funny. A few crossed the street to proceed on the other side. Being in an excellent mood, I smiled and waved at them. Suddenly, I realized that I was barefoot. Then I noticed I was still wearing my pajamas.

This outfit was clearly not in compliance with the office dress code. To say the least.

I kept going, but now I was starting to wonder if Henry's advice was right. Could I really trust him after all the abuse he had suffered at my hands as a young kid on the farm?

Maybe a day at work on LSD, or whatever it was that I had ingested, was not such a good idea after all. I decided to stop and think about it. By now I was across the street from my office. Looking around the area, I noticed a beautiful tree overlooking the sidewalk. I thought to myself, "I'll just climb up that tree and think this whole situation over."

Up the tree I went. I found a nice comfy limb with a view and began watching all the people heading in to work. They seemed like machines in a Charlie Chaplin film.

Suddenly I saw Robert coming up the street below the tree. Impulsively I said, "Hi Bob." He looked around, left and right and behind him, but he didn't see me. I said "Up here. In the tree." Finally he glanced up and saw me sitting there, barefoot and in my pajamas. I waved. Realizing that I probably needed to say something more, but not knowing how best to explain the situation, on the spur of the moment I said, "I don't think I am going in to work today."

Robert replied, after a moment of thought, "That seems like a good idea." He waved and went on his way to the office. I stayed in the tree a while, watching the pedestrian traffic, and then went back home.

When I got home, Henry said, "How did it go?"

I said, "You little jerk! You didn't tell me I was still in my pajamas! I could have been fired."

I didn't get fired. Robert never mentioned the incident, and I never knew what he thought. In fact, to my knowledge, he never said one word about this strange event, right up to the day he died. We remained good friends for decades, and I realized that he was a rare treasure—a person who could be trusted to keep confidence about anything.

Despite my appreciation for Robert saving me from losing my job, I soon realized that the confining life of ties and coats in a small, insular law office was not my cup of tea at this formative stage of my young life. I had been living the same lifestyle I lived when in law school, which is to say in abject poverty—even though I was now making a decent salary. My $25-a-month rent in a slum apartment, plus groceries, did not make even a noticeable dent in my income. I realized that I had saved thousands in just a year. I näively concluded it was enough to retire.

I am reminded of the story Kurt Vonnegut told of his visit with Joseph Heller to a party of rich Wall Street types at an exclusive Shelter Island mansion. Vonnegut asked Heller if he realized that their host, a hedge fund manager, made more money in a single day than Heller made from his wildly popular novel, *Catch-22*, over its whole history. Heller replied, "Yes, but I have something he will never have." "What is that?" asked Vonnegut. Heller replied, "I have enough."[13]

I realized that I had saved enough to follow my dreams of exotic travel and other adventures and that, if I continued working in the legal profession, those would be reduced to an annual one-week vacation in Cancun.

So I quit that job and took off on several years of adventures around the world.

---

[13] This widely cited story is based on Kurt Vonnegut, "Joe Heller" (poem), *The New Yorker*, May 16, 2005.

6

HITTING THE ROAD

Tourists don't know where they've been, travelers don't know where they're going.
—Paul Theroux

Traveling is a zone of life which presents vast opportunities for making mistakes. Especially if the travel is in Third World countries and places with little or no government as we know it. Even more opportunities arise if the traveler does not know where he or she is, or why he or she is there, and does not speak a word of the language.

WHERE'S HENRY?

"Where IS Henry?" That's the question my mother asked me time and time again after my younger brother Henry disappeared. I don't know why she thought I would know. I had no idea.

Henry had joined the Peace Corps to avoid the Vietnam War. Young Americans were coming back in body bags, plane load after plane load. So to many boys his age, just out of college, the Peace Corps offered a way out, a draft deferment. Henry ended up in a small African country named Malawi. That was fine, my mother thought: "He is probably helping people, and at least he is not getting shot."

I knew better. I knew he was going to get into hot water wherever he was because that was what he did. It was in his DNA.

After a while, our mother stopped getting letters from Africa. Months went by. Eventually, she got a letter from Henry, postmarked London, England, requesting that she send him some money via American Express in London. She called me up and said, "You have got to go find Henry. He seems to have left the Peace Corps and is now somewhere in England." Always an obedient lad, I got her to float me a round-trip ticket to London and started off on the search. I had nothing better to do.

But where to start? I chose American Express in London, where he had instructed mother to send him cash. Sure enough, they gave me an address: Clipstreet Farmhouse, Norwich, Norfolk. Off I went to a remote farming area off the coast of the North Sea. It was not exactly a resort area. It rained all the time. There were no attractions that I could discern. I was curious as to how he had landed there.

After wandering around Norfolk for a while asking questions about where Clipstreet might be, a postman finally directed me to the address. It was a quiet old stone and brick farmhouse with a yard full of weeds (which later turned out to be edible). I knocked on the door. A young lady, all wrapped up in blankets to fight off the cold streaming in from the North Sea, answered and said, "Yes. He is in the other room getting a fire started. Who are you?" I explained who I was and why I was there. She said, "I am Pippa." Nice name, I thought. I found her friendly and attractive, despite being bundled up in five layers of clothing.

Henry was indeed in the next room, breaking up furniture and throwing it in the fireplace. The house had no heat, and they had no coal or wood. It was not their house, so into the fire went the furniture.

Henry and Pippa were both a bit impecunious at that time, with little cash between them. They were subsisting on tea and the weeds in the garden, which turned out to be rhubarb. Not bad, though monotonous. Pippa was married to the guy who owned the house, David. He was the heir to a manure/fertilizer company fortune, and had bought the house for him and Pippa to live in, but then he decided that he was gay and disappeared. Henry's girlfriend had also flown the coop, back to Vancouver, Canada.

I was welcomed into the Clipstreet scene by both of them, since it was clear that I had more money than they did. I actually had only a few hundred dollars to my name, but I had a credit card given to me by a large New York bank when I graduated from law school. I guess they figured that anyone who graduated from Harvard Law School was a good bet for a credit card. Wrong thinking on their part. It was only after two years of wild spending and no payments that they cancelled the card and began trying to retrieve the loot I had spent all over the U.S., England, and the rest of Europe.

The Clipstreet scene was slow. We sat around smoking hash that Henry had brought back from North Africa after being dismissed from his Peace Corps post. We killed time eating rhubarb, drinking tea, and occasionally visiting the local pub to play darts. Someone had the idea that we could jazz things up a bit by taking a road trip to a warm place with beaches. Portugal sounded good, but we needed transportation.

Pippa found an allegedly trustworthy used-car salesman who promised to bring us a reliable car right to the farm, right away. I knew that the term "trustworthy used-car salesman" was an oxymoron, but he showed up, and I took a chance. I forked over most of the cash I had left. That was a bad decision. The car was a wreck. But it did start and moved around the flatlands of Norfolk. We took it on a test drive to a little shore town, Cromer, which was famous for its crabs. The car seemed ok.

Off we went, destination Portugal.

After visiting some of Pippa's friends in London, and sharing Henry's hash with them (he had a sizable block), we took off for the Dover-to-Calais ferry. Sadly, the ramp from the street up to the ferry was more of a hill than our brand-new car could manage. It had no power. No compression. A pitiful transmission. The ferry hands had no time for our mechanical issues. They pushed the car up the ramp and went on about their business.

This did not bode well for the rest of the trip. There was no way we were going to find flat roads with no hills between Calais and Portugal. In fact, there were mountains in the way.

We drove the car as far as we could across the flat coastal plain of France until we came to the first hill. The broken-down jalopy could not make it up the hill. We took the tags off and left it on the side of the road.

We caught a ride to the city of Le Mans, where we found a car rental agency willing to rent us a car based on my credit card. We signed the papers and headed south.

Pippa did not have a driver's license, and in fact, had never learned to drive. I hated driving, so that left the driving to Henry. We wanted to drive straight though, nonstop, so somehow we had to keep Henry awake. Pippa had the solution: a quick trip to the Pharmacia. She sauntered boldly up to the counter and ordered "dexedrina spansule." She got a bottle of little black pills, known in the U.S.A. as "black beauties." We kept them on the dashboard and told Henry to take one whenever he started to doze off. They kept him wide awake, bug-eyed, and going strong at the wheel for two days and three nights nonstop.[14]

We made it to the beaches in Spain just across the border from Portugal and watched some Portuguese fireworks as soon as we got there. Portuguese people are always shooting off fireworks. They love them.

On the trip to Portugal, we treated the car rather cruelly. It was a relatively nice new car when we started, but by the time we got back,

---

[14] Henry, a person who is far from religious, claims to have been outraged by the behavior of Pippa and me in the car. He provided an addition to this story: "There were some other events on that trip that you failed to mention, such as what you and Pippa were doing in the back seat as I drove through the crowded square at the church of Santiago de Compostela in front of the worshippers coming out of the most sacred church in all Spanish Christendom . . . and the disgraceful things you and Pippa were doing at the beach in the sand depression with ALL the neighborhood kids lined up on the banks watching."

it was a mess. We hit every bump and pothole in the worst roads of rural Spain until finally the car's suspension was nothing but mush. It looked bad too—so bad that when we returned to the rental shop in France, we waited until closing time, parking the car across the street. When I saw the manager lock the door I ran up and gave him the keys, saying we were late for the ferry. We high-tailed it out of town and to the coast to catch the ferry out of the country.

We could not hitchhike in a group of three, so Pippa and I had to separate from Henry. At the ferry terminal, we could not find Henry. I thought to myself, "I have failed. My mission was to find Henry and convince him to go home. Now he is lost again, and I am going home empty-handed."

At the last minute Henry showed up. It was a good thing too, because he had absolutely no money, and I needed to buy him a ticket. All's well that ends well, as they say, but it was worrisome. He was still traveling with nothing much but a sizable block of hash. If caught with that, it would have been jail time.

An additional note: Henry asserts that Pippa and I stayed at hotels on the trip, but that we never let him in. He claims that he had to sleep in the car. He still seems bitter about that. He also asserts that Pippa and I made no effort to find him at the ferry because we went out to dinner, emerging at the ferry entrance at the last minute, causing him a great deal of anxiety. I have no memory at all of any of those events. Henry had been eating a lot of black beauties on the trip, and I suspect he may have been hallucinating.

In fact, all three of us each have different memories of this trip, possibly because of the mix of hash and black beauties we were indulging in. Pippa claims, for example, that I did most of the driving. That memory seems dubious even to me. But who knows?

A HICK FROM MARYLAND DOES NOT BELONG IN NORTH AFRICA

Travel is glamorous only in retrospect.
—Paul Theroux

Our rickety Yugoslavian cargo vessel docked in Casablanca. I got off the boat with my girlfriend, Pippa Collingwood (who I later married). We started looking for a place to stay. I glanced around the unfamiliar waterfront and saw all the Berbers and Tuaregs and Muslim women in black veils. I thought to myself, with a bit of discomfort, "Where am I? What the hell have I gotten myself into?" I was not in Sykesville, Maryland, anymore.

I had resigned from my government job as a lawyer in Congress with some money in my pocket, and I was ready for a different life. Two years of difficult legal work, wearing a coat and tie every day, was—I figured—enough to last me a lifetime.

Traveling with my English girlfriend, Pippa, was definitely different. I had met her in England when I went there at my mother's request, looking for my brother Henry.

Pippa had a posh accent but she was an honest-to-goodness, old-school European hippie. She had a Ph.D. in Hippiness. I was just along for the ride because I was fascinated by her and by the hippie lifestyle she wanted me to blend into. She was the driving force behind this trip (and our later trip to Woodstock, described in another story in this book).

I blended more or less awkwardly into the hippie culture for a while, with scraggly hair down to my butt and a joint always hanging from my lips, but in the end, I could never make a permanent commitment to that lifestyle. On the other hand, for a couple of years, being out on the road with hundreds of other stoned-to-the-gills dropouts was a really wild experience for a naïve farm boy.

As a small child living on an isolated farm, I became fascinated with the pictures and stories from hundreds of old National Geographic magazines that my parents had accumulated over the years. I was not much interested in the stories about America or Europe, but the photographs of far-off exotic places thrilled me. I longed to go to a place like the Sahara Desert or the Himalayan Mountains and see those weird and strange sights up close. I was primed and ready when Pippa suggested a trip to Morocco.

It was the early 1970s, and we were in our 20s, young and careless. We were both interested in seeing the world and agreed that Third World travel was the way to go. Cheap. Exotic. This particular trip began in Norfolk, Virginia, where we boarded a beat-to-hell Yugoslavian freighter bound for Casablanca.

The idea was to take the cheapest cargo ship we could find to Casablanca and then visit all the hippie hot spots in the rest of the country. There we could try out the various varieties of hasheesh legally available there, and hang out with all the other cool European hippies. Then we would somehow move on across North Africa and the Middle East, and finally across Pakistan and India to Kathmandu.

There were several hippie hotspots in Morocco. Marrakech, of course, but the wildest one was Essaouira on the coast. In Essaouira, to the consternation of local Moroccans, European hippies wandered around the beach naked and stoned out of their minds. Some lived in trees. Others slept on the beach under the stars. All the big British rock and roll bands visited, including the Rolling Stones. To Pippa, Essaouira sounded like the place to be. I was curious myself.

I was not well travelled, to say the least. I spent my youth on a farm in Howard County, Maryland, milking cows and bailing hay, seldom going beyond the tiny nearby village of Sykesville. Eventually, I went to high school in the city of Baltimore, and then to a straight-laced college and law school, both in east coast American cities.

I was basically a hick. Going to an exotic foreign place like Morocco was mind-blowing for me. Pippa, on the other hand, had grown up in Istanbul and spent years in London. She had travelled all over the world by the time we hooked up. She planned to cure me of my provincialism, and I was looking forward to the cure.

The rust-bucket freighter Pippa booked for our trip was barely seaworthy. There were fewer than a dozen passengers, including us. It was a rickety operation, but ridiculously cheap. Pippa was into cheap. She was the ultimate low-budget traveler.

The other passengers on the ship were true-blue California hippies of the extreme variety. Later in life, they probably all became Silicon Valley billionaires, but they were definitely in an earlier and looser phase at the time they were on the boat. I had never before seen this extreme variety of hippie on the east coast. They looked like escapees from the Grateful Dead or Ken Kesey's bus. They were dropping acid all day and all night, and doing tai chi and yoga on deck at dawn.

Below deck, the female California hippies carried out their commitment to free love by engaging in sex with the Yugoslavian crew, who had never before enjoyed anything like this aboard a vessel. And those sailors had seen a lot. The crew lined up for the nightly free love. One middle-aged passenger, a woman from San Francisco, was a high-school teacher on the lam from the law with one of her students, a 17-year-old, crazy, tripped-out young dude. In that couple, I never figured out who had seduced whom before they got run out of the high school and had to flee California. I was impressed by her stamina, however. She had sex below deck multiple times with the entire crew, except the captain.

We docked in Casablanca, Morocco. That was where the even more strange adventures began.

I quickly found that Pippa's favored mode of international travel was hitchhiking and staying in the cheapest imaginable, filthy, flea-bag places. In Morocco, flea bags were really bad news. Some of them were noisy whorehouses and all were stunningly filthy. All had only holes in the floor for toilets. We had large bugs and rats crawling over us at night. But we never paid more than $3 a night!

I got sick from the street food, which was all we ate. It was all we could afford on our budget. To fix me up, Pippa brought in a local witch doctor who chanted some stuff and rubbed a stinky oil on me. It cost about $2 and failed to effect a cure. I did not recover for a week.

Pippa's fundamental mission was to make our cash last as long as possible. We started with about $2,000, and she made it last for two years. We covered fifteen countries and about 25,000 miles. Must be some kind of record for low-budget travel.

In Marrakech, while I was lying sick as a dog in a whorehouse, Pippa wandered around town and came across a movie being made called *Babylon*. Part of the film involved an orgy around a campfire. Pippa got a part as an extra in the orgy. It must have been fun because she still talks about it, although she never mentioned it to me at the time.

After seeing all the sights in Marrakech and other major Moroccan hippie hangouts, and smoking legendary quantities of hash in each and every one, we decided to cross the desert and check out the pyramids in Egypt. We thought a camel might be the cheapest way to do the desert part of that trip; so we headed south to a famous camel market near the border with Spanish Sahara. Our idea was to buy a reliable second-hand camel.

I am not sure that we were thinking clearly. You could even say we were stupid. Or naïve. Or foolish. All of that may be true, but the camel plan seemed really good after smoking a block of Moroccan hash.

We were the only Europeans or Americans at the camel market, and it quickly became clear that we were not going to get a good deal. Everyone was trying to cheat us. And the camels stank to hell. They all had bad breath. They were also given to trying to bite any unwary humans within reach.

Camel market at Goluimine

So the plan was revised. Forget the camel. Forget the Sahara Desert. We found a bus that would take us north across the Atlas Mountains and then east to Algeria, one country closer to Egypt and the fabled pyramids. Before we hopped on the bus, Pippa decided that we should take some pills to make the trip more beautiful. The pills hit pretty quick. I thought the bus ride was hilarious. The other passengers must have thought we had some sort of laughing disease. At one point on the bus ride, we decided we needed to get off the bus and get the full experience of the Moroccan desert. We asked the bus driver to drop us off at the next town.

We got off the bus and looked around. Nothing but bare sand desert. The bus driver pointed in one direction and indicated that we should hike off there. So we took off on foot across the barren Sahara. Soon a ravine appeared. Down inside was a little village of mud huts. This looked pretty good. We were still totally stoned and sauntered right in. The people down in the canyon were very nice. Someone found a bed in a house for us to sleep in. We were definitely objects of curiosity.

Next day, back out on the road, we caught another bus going over the Atlas Mountains. Soon we were in Algeria. Hitchhiking in a Muslim country was not that well received. Nevertheless, we persisted. We made it through Algiers and kept going east. We got run out of one village by stone-throwing women because Pippa forgot to fully cover her head.

Eventually, with the help of an Algerian Army officer who told us we were going to get killed if we kept hitchhiking, we made it to the Tunisian border. He drove us part of the way in his military vehicle. We caught a bus the rest of the way.

Unfortunately, there was trouble at the border. The border guards decided to search the bus for drugs because there were a few other hippies on board with us. One terrified dude threw his stash out the window, but there was enough residue in his pocket to result his being pulled off the bus. Pippa, of course, was not going to let a nice stash go to waste, so as soon as the border guard left, she found the stash in the grass and saved it for our future enjoyment.

Tunisia was wonderful. A lot of French speakers wanted to talk with us. I was picking up a little French by then, so we could communicate a bit. Pippa had heard that all the cool hippies went to the exquisite little island of Djerba on the Tunisian coast. Of course, there we went.

Djerba was idyllic. We met a couple of German acid heads who were going back to Munich. They gave us their beach house to live in, and a nice supply of LSD. They also wanted to have group sex with us, but I was too shy to try that.

We left Tunisia for Egypt, but first we had to go through Libya. King Idris, unbeknownst to us, had just been deposed by Muammar al-Qaddafi, and fighting was still going on. At the Tunisia-Libya border, we were refused entry. We needed to revise the travel plan again.

We headed to London by way of a ferry boat to Marseilles, followed by more hitchhiking through France. I was getting tired of the relentless hitchhiking and wanted to buy a car in London for the next long trip ahead. This time, we set our sights on the ultimate hippie destination: Kathmandu.

When we got to London we hooked up with some of Pippa's friends and, of course, smoked a lot of pot. Meanwhile I was looking for a car. I finally settled on a small English Anglia delivery van that was being resuscitated by some Pakistani guys in the East End. This, I thought, we could sleep in safely. They had allegedly refurbished the engine. The price was $200 American.

With this vehicle, we felt we were ready to travel all the way to Kathmandu by way of Europe, Turkey, Iran, Afghanistan, Pakistan, and India. This is a route no one in their right mind would attempt today, but back in the early 1970s there was a constant stream of European hippies on that route. It was known then as the "Hippie Trail."

Off we went on the second leg of our great adventure. It was about

20,000 miles by road round trip, and some of the roads were basically rutted dirt trails. This was going to be a real test of the skills and honesty of the Paki mechanics who sold us the van.

Next up, adventures on the Hippie Trail.

LOST WHITE BOY IN SEARCH OF ENLIGHTENMENT

> *Perhaps there are two kinds of people: those for whom nothingness is no problem, and those for whom it is an insuperable problem.*
> —John Updike, *Self-Consciousness*, 2012

After our trip to Egypt ended ignominiously at the Libyan border, thanks to Colonel Qaddafi, my travel partner, Pippa, and I found ourselves in London, still not cured of the travel bug. We came up with a new plan to take the Hippie Trail from London to either Goa or Kathmandu, or possibly both. Those were the favored hippie destinations. As described in the story of our North African trip, we had decided to buy a vehicle for this expedition. I was fed up with hitchhiking and buses, and this route we were planning was a formidable one.

Meanwhile, I had developed an itch for enlightenment. I was on a search for wisdom, the meaning of life...or something. Like so many people in the 1970s, I found materialistic life in America and Europe completely unsatisfying. Shopping malls? Working in an office every day for eight hours or more? Big Macs for lunch? Traffic jams? Goodness gracious! That couldn't be all there was to life. After a few pharmaceutical voyages, and a lot of reading about Eastern religions and the spirituality of making a direct connection to the unknowable, the so-called "reality" of everyday life in a corporation or law firm seemed like a living death. A lot of other people were also looking for something else.

I had become fascinated with various Eastern religions, particularly Sufism. Sufism is the mystical side of Islam, feared and hated by traditional Islamic religious leaders because it offers a direct pipeline to God. Sufis have to live underground in strict Islamic countries. I was also reading the great teachers of mysticism, Gurdjieff and Ouspensky, and had become a fan of their curious magical teaching. It was a long way from Christianity.

All humans crave meaning and purpose. Most are lost without it. Usually, they just take what they can from their parents and community in the form of religion of one kind or another. It's a quick and easy solution, one which solves the difficult problem of figuring things out for yourself or going on a long pilgrimage to find a teacher. Others decide to look into the matter more deeply. They start searching.

Some people cannot tolerate the notion that life is meaningless and without purpose. If the religious tradition they were brought up in fails to click for them, off they go on a (usually futile) search to find their purpose and the "true" meaning of life. Sometimes they end up in a cult or right back in the religion they started with. A few brave souls begin to realize the reality of the human situation and accept that there is no extrinsic purpose or meaning in our lives. You have to create it.

The idea that answers to the mysteries of life can be found in religious systems, in cults, or even in esoteric spiritual quests, is a dangerous one. I did not realize it, but I was at a perilous inflection point in my life. I was on the verge of a huge, life-changing mistake. If I had found the "answer" in a guru's ashram somewhere in India or Nepal, I might still be there singing "om mani padme hum" or some such chant for the rest of my life.

I had long ago lost my connection to the Christian religion that I had been brought up in. Sitting in church one day, bored out of my skull and repeating for the umpteenth time the Apostles Creed, "I believe in the Father, Son, and Holy Ghost, etc., etc.," I suddenly realized that I didn't believe any of that stuff. I had no idea who the Holy Ghost was. Moreover, I did not care. Whatever I believed, it was not that. I was stuck in a spiritual wasteland.

My search was on for the meaning of life. I was not alone. Millions of Americans and Europeans were disillusioned with the ridiculous, childish stories in the Bible or Torah and believed that the real answers and ultimate truth could be found in the East. That was where the gurus came from, after all, and gurus acted like they had all the answers. I was another version of what was referred to in the 1970s as "a lost white boy in search of enlightenment."

In the late 1960s and early 1970s, gurus were proliferating all over Europe and America. They came in a great variety. Some were rather odd fellows, such as Meher Baba, who had not said a word for 35 years. At least it was easy to understand him without knowing Sanskrit. He used a chalkboard and was very reassuring. His major message was "Don't worry. Be happy." Others seemed mainly involved in collecting Rolls Royces and young female followers. Some were involved in magic tricks. It was hard to tell who was authentic and who was not.

My first serious connection with Eastern spiritual teaching was with Transcendental Meditation (TM). I went to a meeting with the Maharishi, near my home in Washington, D.C. I did lots of chanting, obtained a personal mantra, and learned how to properly meditate. That stayed with me over the years. It's a useful skill, I have to admit. I still meditate using the TM system.

TM was the real deal, and it should have been enough. But I felt that I needed to go to the physical source, wherever that was, and find a personal teacher. I thought Sufis probably had the answer, but it could be the Buddhists, or maybe one of the exotic Hindu gurus.

Sufis were hard to find because they were suppressed by Islam. They had to hide out from the ayatollahs.

Hinduism is the most ancient, fascinating, and funny one of all the Eastern religions. It was colorful and sexy. There were dozens of Hindu gurus on the loose. Most of them could do magical things and read people's minds. The exceptional ones mostly stayed quietly out of sight, especially when westerners showed up. They probably did not relish becoming the subject of an article in Rolling Stone magazine featuring a British rock and roll band.

Some former leaders of the LSD movement, like Richard Alpert, later Baba Ram Dass, transitioned completely to being followers of a spiritually powerful guru. In Ram Dass's case it was Neem Karoli Baba, known as Maharaj-ji. He went in hook, line and sinker with Maharaj-ji for the rest of his life, giving up LSD (largely), lecturing, and writing dozens of books about love and spirituality.

Back to the geographical part of my spiritual search.

It began in London with the little Anglia van I bought from some Pakistani mechanics. To get used to living in a small van, Pippa and I first went to a little rural music festival held in a cow pasture, similar to Woodstock. (It has now become the big and famous Glastonbury Festival, bigger than Woodstock was.) Then we were off to Scotland and the Isle of Mull to visit Rosie, Pippa's sister. I don't remember much about Mull other than ending up in a ditch outside of a cèilidh (Scottish dance party). I had been tossed out of the party with another drunken young lad who was teaching me how to consume the local whiskey in traditional quantities.

Soon Pippa and I took off on the main journey. We blasted through most of Europe in the little white van as quickly as possible, because there were clearly no exotic places or spiritual answers to be found anywhere in modern capitalist Europe. The roads in Germany and Switzerland were excellent, but we hit some rough patches getting across the mountains in Yugoslavia (a country that no longer exists) to Greece.

The little Anglia van was still running when we got to Istanbul. Istanbul was almost Pippa's home territory. She had grown up there when her father was in the British Navy. So Istanbul was a lengthy stop, visiting her old haunts and eating the food that she loved. Lots of eggplant. Again I got sick from the street food. That made for an even longer delay, but what the hell? We didn't have any schedule anyway.

In the twenty-first century, traveling around the world and living full time in a small vehicle is still a lifestyle for a few hardy souls. But it is now way more dangerous than it was in the 1960s when Pippa and I drove one from Europe to Nepal.

Our first breakdown was on a remote dirt road east of Istanbul and west of Ankara. Turkish mechanics, using Russian parts, came to the rescue.

Turkey was not my favorite place, but then we never went to the coast or to the north, the most fascinating and beautiful parts. We were on a beeline for India and Nepal. We did see the whirling dervishes in Istanbul. They were supposed to be Sufis who whirled themselves into religious ecstasy. That did not appeal to me much, and the ones we saw were clearly paid tourist attractions, not real Sufi mystics.

We rolled into Iran and visited some stunning spots there, including some awesome mosques. The cities in Iran were open and westernized then, in the pre-Ayatollah days. The CIA was still in charge via its puppet Shah. Everyone was pretty relaxed before he got run out of the country. We ate fabulous chelo kebab (rice and lamb kebab) with yogurt from street vendors every day. That dish is still, to this day, my favorite meal.

Afghanistan was even more fascinating and had a lot less western influence. It was not yet on the CIA's radar. Afghani men were mostly giants, with rifles and horses. Tough guys. The country was basically populated by a rough bunch of tribes, loosely held together by a king. Things were not all that organized, as we quickly discovered.

We made it to the Iran-Afghanistan border too late in the day to cross, so we parked the van near the crossing and went to sleep. During the night a whole gang of Afghanis on horses rode through, not bothering with the border formalities, shooting up the little border guards' building and putting a few bullets through the wall next to our van. Luckily they missed hitting me or Pippa. I am sure they had no idea that the parked van was occupied by two clueless sleeping westerners.

That was our introduction to Afghanistan. Everything was very loose there. Hippies loved the place because hash and other drugs were everywhere and were incredibly cheap and pure. The black opiated hash was their favorite, stamped with the king's insignia to prove its quality. A lot of European and American hippies never got any farther on the trail than Kabul because, if it was drugs you were after, Afghanistan had them all.

Pippa and I were on a larger mission, however. We left Afghanistan when we learned that Jimi Hendrix had died. That event threw the entire hippie community into a conniption fit. Everyone was depressed, and opium and heroin became the answer. Hendrix was as near to a god to them as anyone. Everyone was moping around, overdosing on one drug or another.

Before we left the country, the king staged a Buzkashi game. This was not to be missed. It was the Afghan version of polo, played with a greased dead calf instead of a polo ball. While the king watched, two teams of the strongest horsemen in the country tried to pick up the greased calf from the ground, haul it up on one of their huge horses, and throw it into the other team's goal, which was just a wooden box or something like that.

It was insane.

The problem for the spectators was that there were no clear boundaries and no stands to sit in or hide behind. When a group of large horsemen came galloping toward you, one dragging a calf and the other group trying madly to wrest it away from him, any spectator in the way had to run for his life—or be trampled to death. All the Afghani spectators knew what to do, but the totally stoned American and European hippies, like me and Pippa, did not pick up on it fast enough. Some people got run over.

We took off for Pakistan, motoring through the infamous Khyber Pass, reported to be filled with bandits and thieves of all kinds. Somehow, we made it safely into Pakistan and kept on going east. Pakistan, even then, was not a place to dally. Lots of grumpy people dressed in black.

It was a relief to get to India, where the women had faces and wore bright colors. No more moaning from the muezzins at mosques all day and all night. People seemed remarkably happier the moment we crossed the Pakistan-India border.

In little villages, everyone was curious about our van. Teachers would let children out of school so they could gather around and stare at us as if we had come from another planet, which of course we had—the Weird Planet of the Western Hippies.

Everywhere we went I was checking for gurus to see if I could find one who could lead me to the path to nirvana. When Richard Alpert got fired from Harvard and Stanford and made his way to India, he easily found dozens of gurus all over the place. He just stumbled into them. In his books, *Be Here Now* and *Being Ram Dass*, he tells about how he would give the gurus LSD to see what happened to them. In one case, he gave a guru 915 micrograms of pure acid. (A normal dose would be about 30 micrograms or less.) This particular guru never blinked an eye. He just said "nice medicine" and went on with his daily meditations. Even Alpert was impressed. And he had probably done more acid by that time than anyone else on the planet other than his Harvard pal, Tim Leary.

Even though Dr. Alpert and I were both on our search in India at roughly the same time, I didn't have any LSD to give away. I did not know as many other spiritual seekers as he did. I wasn't having the kind of luck Alpert had in finding serious gurus. And the street food was making me horribly sick. So Pippa and I decided to head to the mountains.

Off to Kathmandu we went, over the Himalayas in our valiant little van. At the higher altitudes the van would just die, stalling out for lack of oxygen. But it would eventually start up again and soon enough we rolled into Kathmandu Valley, the home away from home for about a million European and American hippies at that time. The food hygiene there was even worse than in India. I was so sick most of the time that I could not even think about searching for gurus or ancient wisdom. Instead I searched for the nearest flush toilet.

We drove up to the Chinese border and stared through the fence at the Chinese soldiers in their little Mao hats and dark green uniforms with the red star. There were little round stupas all over Nepal surrounded by prayer flags, but without a teacher to tell me what to do, I was finding it hard to stay focused on my spiritual mission. It didn't help that all the street restaurants were serving hash brownies, so in addition to being sick from the food, I was generally stoned all day and into the next, when the pattern repeated itself.

After one particularly bad bout with a fever and stomach illness, I decided it was time to turn around and head back to India. Actually, I was getting homesick, as well as being physically sick most of the time.

Back in India, I continued to look half-heartedly for a guru. I was fortunate to find a spiritual leader in a temple who seemed like he might be the real deal. Finally! I thought. He asked me a lot of questions about what I was doing and what I was looking for. After several hours of exhausting interrogation, he said to me, "Mr. Barrow, I have some advice for you. You should stop this search right now, go home, and get a job. You are not ready for this kind of thing, and you probably never will be."

I agreed with this particular guru. I was not cut out to be a spiritual person. I felt like I was in a Cheech and Chong movie, bowing down on my hands and knees, claiming to the spiritual master that "I am not worthy. I am not worthy." Over and over again.

I told Pippa what the guru had said and that I wanted to go home and do something boring and "normal" again. She was a little grumpy about that idea at first, but I think she was also a bit fatigued with my guru search. She still longed to go to Goa, however. We still had a couple hundred dollars left and we had not been to Goa, the place of Pippa's fantasies, where hippies congregated, where we could stay stoned 24/7, and where we could run around naked on the beach. But I wasn't so much into all that anymore. I was depressed about not finding a spiritual leader who wanted me as a follower, and I was physically weak from vomiting and diarrhea. I weighed about 120 pounds, 30 or 40 pounds less than when I left home.

It was clear to me by now that the Eastern spiritual path was not going to be my path. Pippa understood that. I convinced her to drop the Goa dream and we headed back west across Pakistan and into Afghanistan in our little, increasingly feeble, Anglia van.

The van had been through a lot by this time and was acting

up. I knew it would never make it all the way back to England. We went down to the big open-air market in Kabul and started selling everything in the van. You could sell anything and everything there in that big outdoor market. You could probably have sold your dirty underpants. After we had sold everything in the van, even the pencils, we sold the van itself. We made enough money for a bus ticket to Munich.

We got on one of the big German buses that went straight through, nonstop, Kabul to Munich and back several times a week. We were back in Europe in less than 3 days and 3 long nights.

My spiritual journey was over. The physical traveling part, anyway.

I came back from that trip with a tiny nugget of wisdom—that a spiritual quest for a teacher was not my bag, especially if a god or some superior outside force was involved. I was much more comfortable with meditation on my mantra and living with the notion that life is empty and meaningless. That way, I could fill in the empty blanks however I wanted. That, I think, is what's called self-actualization. Or you can call it whatever you want.

Too Deep in the Jungle

As you may have deduced from some of the previous stories, I liked to travel when I was young, and I was not particularly interested in tourist spots. It was the more remote mountains and deserts that attracted me; possibly due to reading too many old National Geographic magazines as a young boy. At one point, I realized that I had never been to the jungle. That oversight needed fixing.

The biggest and most remote uncharted jungle seemed to be the Amazon River basin. But how to get there?

A bit of research suggested that one could get deep into the Amazon through Brazil, Colombia, or Venezuela. I thought, why not visit all three? I found a place called Leticia where the three countries bordered each other. It was on the banks of the Amazon River, inaccessible by road, and deep in the jungle. My kind of place.

My companion, Pippa, was up for an adventure and so we set off to see if we could get to Leticia. We flew to Bogota, Colombia, and visited some of the coastal areas of Columbia, including the beautiful historic city of Cartagena and the nasty, crime-infested port of Barranquilla. All along we were asking about how to get to Leticia. Mostly, no one had ever heard of it. No one, "nada persona," went there, we were told. That definitely piqued my interest.

The search ended when we found that a military plane made sporadic trips to Leticia to maintain what passed for law and order in that part of the Amazon region. We begged and pleaded and finally got a ride on that plane from Bogota down into the heart of darkness. The plane had no seats, just some cargo—mostly boxes of Cheetos which were apparently beloved by the natives of the jungle—and a few scraggly soldiers who had pulled jungle duty.

The soldiers were supposed to monitor and stop smuggling across the Venezuelan, Brazilian, and Colombian borders in the jungle. Fat chance! Leticia was a smugglers' paradise. Law enforcement was nonexistent because the soldiers knew better than to mess with the situation there.

Leticia was a one-street town, one block of which was actually paved. It consisted of bars and weapons stores, together with numerous pens and cages of wild animals and birds which had been caught and were awaiting shipment down the river and, ultimately, to wealthy collectors in Europe and Asia. We were definitely out of place. We kept a low profile.

There was not a lot to do in Leticia, if you were not a smuggler or escaped convict. We spent some time on the banks of the Amazon. It was about the only place you could go without being bitten, stung, or eaten by some jungle creature. One day we noticed a hairy individual meandering down the river in a dugout canoe. It was a 20-year-old white guy. And he spoke English with an Australian accent!

Over a few beers in one of the local pubs, the Aussie guy told us his story. He was on a "walkabout," which is a thing Australians often do when they start to mature. They got the idea from the aborigines, who also did walkabouts when they reached maturity, albeit in the Australian outback. The white Australians took the tradition all the way around the world. This particular fellow decided to go from the headwaters of the Amazon River in Peru all the way down to the Atlantic in a dugout canoe. He was about halfway when we met him. Already he had experienced enough close calls and dangerous encounters of every imaginable kind to fill two books.

After meeting this character, I remembered something I had read once, probably from a travel writer: "Whenever you have reached the end of the road and think you have arrived at the harshest, most remote, most unforgiving place on the planet, there you will probably find an Australian."

We were not up for the Aussie walkabout. In fact, we were afraid to go off into the dense jungle. But we were bored and disappointed with Leticia. Sadly, our trip ended with an uneventful return to Barranquilla, then home.

ACAPULCO GOLD

The Mexican security guards in the grocery store seemed to come from nowhere. Six of them. They closed in around the three of us with menacing expressions and heavy automatic weapons at the ready. "What the hell is going on?" I felt a sudden panic. "How did we get into this mess?"

Back in the 1960s, when everyone I knew was smoking weed, the top-of-the-line stuff was called "Acapulco Gold." I assumed that meant that it was from Acapulco. At that time I had not been to Mexico yet, but I had seen slick tourist ads showing guys diving off towering cliffs into beautiful, clear, azure water hundreds of feet below.

Both the Acapulco Gold and the diving appealed to me, and the Gold really appealed to my girlfriend at the time, Pippa. Pippa was an English hippie—a special breed of hippie back in the 1960s, into hippie clothing and high-quality dope. I was OK with that, but mainly I wanted to jump off a cliff into deep water.

So we decided to go to Mexico—the first time for both of us. Off we went in my diminutive Fiat, a car with only three cylinders and about 50 horsepower. The gas would not set us back much.

(That little car later took us to Woodstock. We parked it on the road leading to the concert, and walked three miles to get to the hill where we lived in the mud with a couple hundred thousand other people our age for three days. But that's another story.)

Our first stop on the Mexico trip was Chapel Hill, North Carolina, where my two brothers were living, allegedly involved in some way with the university there. They lived together in a two-story concrete block shack. It was disgusting. People came and went continuously and left garbage behind. The yard was a junk-collector's dream.

Most memorable was the kitchen sink. No one had experimented with washing dishes in the eight months they had been living there. Dishes (and who knows what else) were piled in and around the sink, with green mold at least two inches thick on everything. Even a self-respecting rat would have been appalled. We didn't eat anything there.

The parties in Chapel Hill—the Haight-Ashbury of the south— were out of control. They went on 24/7, many of them at an isolated farm near Carrboro. LSD and other hallucinogens were all over the place, all day, every day. It was good stuff—blotter acid supposedly made by Owsley Brown, brought to Chapel Hill by my brother from an artist friend in Los Angeles.

Someone told me that when Janis Joplin came to town for a concert, before she was famous, she wound up at a party in my brothers' place and passed out on a bed upstairs, surrounded by empty liquor bottles. I could easily believe that story.

It was hard to stick to our Mexico mission in the soup of drugs and parties that we got swallowed up in in Chapel Hill. Finally, the horizon cleared, and we decided to get on with our mission.

While packing up the car, we came across Charlie, a close friend of one of my brothers. He asked, "Where are you going?" "Mexico," I replied.

"Always wanted to go there," Charlie mumbled. He seemed hugely hung over. Or maybe just depressed.

"We're leaving now. Come with us if you want."

I was not even slightly surprised when Charlie climbed into the tiny back seat of the Fiat and said, "Let's roll." He was apparently a bit at loose ends at the time.

Down through the south we went, headed for the Mexican border. We stopped in New Orleans, a crazy city where buildings can fall down in the street and the only thing that happens is that lawsuits are filed. I thought to myself, "I've got to come back here someday." And later on, I did. For JazzFest. Zydeco dances. Mardi Gras parades. And more.

In New Orleans on this trip, we ate red beans and rice. Our budget was small—tiny, in fact—but Charlie's seemed close to nonexistent. He was always hungry.

However, I was happy to have Charlie along to share the driving on the long trip to Acapulco. He was good company, and Pippa did not know how to drive. Americans thought that was weird, but if you lived in London like she did, driving a car was practically useless. When she got to America, she was appalled that you couldn't go anywhere without a car. "This place is a madhouse," she complained.

Into Mexico we sped—if you can call the 50-mph top speed of the Fiat speeding—and directly to Acapulco. We were on a mission.

We were not well prepared for Acapulco. The tourist part was too ritzy for our budget, and the Acapulco Gold was nowhere to be found. The local weed was nasty, and for low-budget travelers like us, it was a question of which slummy lodging we would try to sleep in each night.

Charlie did not even have enough money to afford the fleabags and whorehouses Pippa and I were staying in when we were not just sleeping on the beach. So he hung a broken-down hammock on the trees in the yard and slept there. You couldn't sleep much anyway, inside or out, because the mariachi music went on until 4 am every night. It never rained, though, so Charlie's hammock was probably not all that bad. He never complained.

All three of us were hungry, and we decided to hit the grocery store. For Pippa and me, that meant actually buying some groceries with money. For Charlie, "hitting" the grocery store meant something else.

While Pippa and I browsed through the aisles picking up the cheapest crap we could find, Charlie went for the good stuff. Without a grocery cart. Soon, his underpants contained a can of sardines and other expensive items.

Up to the cashier we sauntered, Pippa and me first. We paid our bill and waited for Charlie to pay for the single candy bar he was clutching nervously. As soon as he was through, all three of us were surrounded by five tough-looking Mexican security cops with automatic weapons. They pointed their guns at Charlie's crotch. Sheepishly, Charlie pulled out the sardines and other food.

I thought we were screwed. I was a bit nervous even though Pippa and I had stolen nothing. But we were lucky: the store cops wanted to bargain. This was hopeless with Charlie, however; he had about two pesos left. I started to worry. "We can't leave him rotting in some disgusting jail in Mexico," I thought. "That would be too tough to explain when we get home."

So I started bargaining on his behalf. For a bribe of about $5 U.S., they let us all go. And all eight of us shook hands on the deal.

The next time I went into a Mexican grocery store, I looked up. There was a balcony all the way around the store, with heavily armed security guards peering down. Forget about stuffing food into your underpants in Mexico.

BAJA CALIFORNIA

Years later, when I was a young man with a second wife and a small family, I returned to Mexico. This time, I thought it would be fun to take my two young children on adventurous trips to wild and woolly places.

That idea was misguided, to say the least.

On one occasion, we went camping in the woods of West Virginia. During the night a family of skunks, a mother and six youngsters, came into our tent looking for, I suppose, food. My two kids did not wake up and both parents remained as still as possible for the 20 minutes during which the skunks roamed around, stepping on us and sitting on us. Finally they left as quietly as they had come. Whew!

One of my most ambitious family trips was to take the four of us on a car trip down the coast of Baja California. Back in those days, Baja California was a wild rural place, a slender peninsula on the west coast of Mexico with terrible roads and worse accommodations. Sounded interesting to me. It would be cheap, at least. We could eat fish tacos and camp out to save on food and hotel bills.

It was Christmas time, and I was a horrible Scrooge. I hated all the gifts, and with at least one child still believing in Santa Claus, I knew we would have to live with that big lie as well. To me, Christmas was all about over-consumption, advertising, and corporate America taking over what used to be a religious holiday. Not that I cared about religion, either. The best option was to get out of America.

Off we went to San Diego, a beautiful Southern California paradise. The family just wanted to stay right there and enjoy the beaches, the weather, and the American food. But no. I had it in my demented brain that it would be more exciting and educational to travel down the entire Baja Peninsula of Mexico. Bad idea.

I dragged my wife at the time and our two kids across the border to Tijuana, Mexico, rented a car, and started down the west coast of Baja California. The roads were actually not too bad on the west coast, and the fish tacos were terrific. So we cruised happily south.

The best part was when we visited a fabulous (but now endangered) whale sanctuary at Magdalena Bay. Every year, gray whales travel the longest migration known to exist among mammals, swimming 10,000-14,000 miles from the cold Arctic seas to Mexico's warm-water lagoons and back. The migrating whales stop over in the protected waters of Baja's calving lagoons for the winter months. In these sheltered waters, gray whales are able to give birth, nurse, and mate without fear of predators. We got to go out in small boats and touch the calm mother whales, who were floating in the extremely high-saline environment that they had searched out as the perfect place to give birth. It was incredible!

But all this touristic stuff was getting on my nerves. I wanted to see the harsh desert backcountry I had read so much about. There was one little dirt rut across the peninsula, from the west coast to the nearly deserted east coast on the Gulf of Mexico. That was where I wanted to go.

Despite all kinds of warnings about banditos, snakes, scorpions, tarantulas, drug dealers, and other concerns, off we went. The road lived up to its horrendous reputation. It was a miserable, rutted dirt track more than a road. We never encountered the bandits, drug dealers, snakes, tarantulas, or scorpions, but so many sleeping wild burros were standing in the middle of the road that you could spend hours trying to get them to move. And you could not drive at all at night because you could not see them in time to stop.

Then there were the soldiers with assault rifles at numerous checkpoints along the otherwise deserted road. Someone must be transporting something along that route, I thought.

We finally made it to the east coast of the Baja peninsula. At first it was disappointing. There was nothing there except some scattered, derelict, dry ranches. No towns. No villages. No nothing.

Eventually we found a derelict building that proclaimed itself in signage to be a "hotel." Run-down does not begin to describe this building. A huff and a puff and it would be gone. So we booked some rooms. Worldwide, including in Africa, I have only once seen filthier rooms. No one could sleep on the filthy sagging beds, and everyone got bitten by bedbugs, which then infested our camping gear.

On south we went, our intrepid team begging me to go back to San Diego. But I persisted, trying to teach them what Third World travel is all about: suffering and misery. This is the lesson I had taken away from my other trips, as some of the other stories in this book describe. But slowly the realization dawned on me that middle-class American women and children longing for Christmas gifts are not going to be thrilled about enduring suffering and misery.

One fine day we found a beach to camp on. A few Mexican families were camping there too, so it felt safe. No facilities, however, so the girls had to learn to hide in the bushes and dig holes in the ground to poop in.

Our keys got locked in the car somehow. The family was terrified when I could not get into the car. Would we be stuck here forever? All four of the Mexican men who were at the beach came over when they sensed our distress. One brought a piece of wire and had the door open in seconds. He claimed, as best I could tell with my bad Spanish, that he was a repo man back in Tijuana. What luck! A repo man way out here!

Later that same day, an itinerant barber showed up at the campsite. He was giving cheap haircuts to anyone at the beach—so I and another member of my family decided that we could use a Mexican haircut.

Bad idea. We all got head lice and spent the next month picking the little bugs out of each other's hair.

Luckily, before things went entirely to pieces, we came upon a remote encampment of young Americans in a group called Outward Bound. They were living in the wilderness of Baja California to test their inner mettle and see if they could survive in the rugged coastal desert. You can imagine their surprise when they saw my bedraggled team struggle into their camp. They said something like: "Hey guys, you are lost. The casinos, restaurants, and hotels are 300 miles from where you are, and in the other direction."

But I did not care how far away civilization was. They had kayaks and other boats. The water was clean and beautiful. They had found an oasis on the east coast of Baja. Not only that, but they were willing to loan us kayaks and give us water and soft drinks. We were home free, in my opinion. So there we stayed for a week or so, having a wonderful time, until there was an incident. Sadly, criminals from the mainland came over in boats during the night and stole all the Outward Bound stuff, including their kayaks.

Our game was up when that happened. We headed back home, with a stop in San Diego at a luxury hotel with a swimming pool and fancy restaurant.

Except for their memories of eating delicious spiny lobsters from the Sea of Cortez and fish tacos at the one and only restaurant we found, my kids have never mentioned to me how much fun they had on the trip to Baja California. In fact, they seem not to want to talk about it at all. Go figure.

My daughter, Isabel, made only one comment (very charitable) after reading this story. "I do not think this trip was a success overall, but I do remember those gray whales."

THE LAST OF THE BIG-WAVE BODY SURFERS

> *A man with few friends is only half developed.*
> –Randolph Bourne, "The Excitement of Friendship," *The Atlantic*, December 1912

I have many memories of traveling with my friend Jack. It was never boring. On some occasions, hospital emergency rooms were involved. Sometimes my luck held out; other times, I paid dearly.

Having an interesting travel companion is one of life's great gifts. For me, flexibility and adaptability are critical characteristics in a travel partner, and I have been fortunate in that respect. Over the years I travelled with Jack Hession, it has always been a unique—and unpredictable—experience.

On the other hand, traveling with someone who is not well organized, and who relentlessly gets lost and forgets things, can be a bit too unpredictable. Since I am not always on top of my game either, things tended to come unwound quickly when we were together.

Jack is an unusually durable fellow, able to sustain multiple serious injuries and keep on trucking in ways that few people can match. In remote places, far from any medical care, he has endured a broken ankle from kayaking on the Upper Youghiogheny River, a broken neck from mountain biking, bloodied feet on a remote dirt road on Alaska's Kenai Peninsula, a dislocated shoulder on the Six Mile River, burned feet from a Chilean campfire, and numerous other injuries. Some of these I don't know many details about, because Jack always downplays the damage. Most recently, he was attacked by a wild turkey while mountain biking in California.

What I do know is that Jack is covered in scars. He is frequently seen in a cast or bandages. His pain threshold, as far as I can tell, is so high as to be almost nonexistent. The CIA could do torture tests on him and he probably would not blink an eye, even during the worst waterboarding they could devise.

Jack's adaptability to setbacks is also legendary. Unanticipated incidents never ruffle his calm demeanor. If you want to travel to far-flung places, and if you don't mind the possibility of serious bodily injuries, getting lost in bear country, strange foreign food, and radical changes in plans at the last minute—then traveling with Jack could be just your cup of tea.

The famous author John McPhee tried taking a trip in Alaska with Jack. In his book *Coming into the Country*, McPhee writes about their canoe trip on the Salmon River in a remote backcountry area that is now Alaska's Kobuk Valley National Park. After nearly becoming dinner for a huge grizzly bear with cubs, halfway down the river, Jack suddenly remembered that his vacation time was almost up. Abandoning the famous writer as he canoed downriver, Jack took off alone, paddling in his own boat at high speed down to the bigger Kobuk River. He was headed back to Anchorage and back to work. McPhee, who had been counting on Jack as a river guide, was left scratching his head, saying to himself, "What now?"

I was already aware of Jack's misadventures when I naïvely agreed to an excursion to a surfing destination on the west coast of Mexico.

Why we were in Mexico in the first place is a memory lost to me. Jack thinks it had something to do with helping the Nantahala Outdoor Center find whitewater rivers in the Mexican mountains. If so, we were not much help in that department. Instead we decided to make it a cultural trip, eating Mexican food, listening all night long to deafening Mariachi bands, and attempting to pick up enough Spanish to survive. We got about as far as calling each other "Señor" and saying "muchas gracias" to each other all the time.

We went to Vera Cruz and immediately got sick from the street food. Then to the nude beach on Isla Mujeres, where we got a good laugh at the ridiculous gringo nudists—and got sick from the food. Culturally, we took away from these experiences that Mexican street food can make a person very sick.

Then Jack had the brilliant idea to go to Puerto Escondido on the Pacific coast where, he said, the best surfing waves in Mexico could be found. In his words, he was "the last of the big-wave body surfers." For some reason, I didn't doubt Jack, although I was wondering to myself how many bodily injuries he had endured in his career as a "big-wave body surfer." The fact that he claimed to be the last one alive was telling. (That claim is specious, of course. Big-wave body surfing is alive and well today worldwide.)

Going along with this plan, it turned out, was not one of my better decisions. Puerto Escondido was not easy to get to. We made it as far as Oaxaca, where Jack discovered an obscure airline that flew back and forth daily to Puerto Escondido: Oaxacana Aerolinea.

We got to the airport, bought tickets at the counter, and went up to the roof of the terminal to watch the plane arrive. We were curious to see what kind of aircraft we would be flying in over these remote mountains. It was a 16-seat Twin Otter. The plane came swooping in, barely clearing the mountain tops, and dropped down to cruise in for landing. Landing on the tarmac, one of its wheels hit something, maybe a snoozing armadillo. The aircraft tipped over slightly to the left. Then it tipped more. Its wing hit the tarmac and sheared off.

The emergency airport staff rolled right out and got the passengers off, but we were thinking to ourselves: "This is not a fix-it-with-duct-tape thing, even in Mexico. Hopefully they have a backup plane."

They did not have a backup plane. That plane was the sole asset of Oaxacana Air. When we returned to the ticket counter to get a refund, we discovered that the entire staff (two young ladies) had fled, the counter was closed, and Oaxacana Aerolinea was no more.

We ended up hiring a van and driver with other passengers who had bought tickets on the wingless aircraft, and we endured a long miserable drive over the mountains to Escondido. It was becoming what I now know is a typical Jack Hession trip.

I don't remember many details after that, except the most important one: when we got to Puerto Escondido, there weren't any big waves.

On another trip with me, this time kayaking in Chile, Jack further cemented his reputation. In one town, he disappeared. I, and his other companions, searched the entire town for him. Late that night, he appeared out of nowhere, saying, "Where were you guys?"

On the same trip, he got badly burned at our campfire cooking dinner and developed a bad infection. Next, at the famous Siete Tazas rapids, he accidentally dropped his kayak with all his equipment into the fast-moving river, while climbing down a steep slope. The kayak went over a waterfall that we could not have navigated. Later, he lost his passport and all his money.

These days Jack spends his time mountain biking through the hills of California, looking for wild turkeys to duel with.

So much fun traveling with Jack. Always.

THE DOG ATE MY PASSPORT

I was sent to Kenya by the American government. Some idiot decided that the Kenyan legislature needed to learn how a real democracy ran its legislature. They recruited me because I knew in excruciating detail how the U.S. House of Representatives worked. I was the Legislative Counsel for that august body at the time. Why the Kenyans consented to this obviously patronizing example of neocolonialism remains a mystery to me, but there must have been money in the deal for someone.

There were several problems with this plan, apart from the neocolonialism aspect. First of all, I knew only too well how the U.S.

legislature worked: badly. I would have the unenviable task of making the process look like a model for a benighted Third World country. This was deceptive at best and dangerous at worst. Our legislature, in case you have not heard, is a train wreck.

Clearly, I was not the best propagandist to speed the glorious word about how a democracy should run its legislature. They decided to send me anyway.

Fortunately, the Kenyans in their legislature had no interest whatsoever in learning how we did things, or rather made a mess of things, in the U.S. They ignored me completely. That was the best outcome for everyone, in my opinion. The Kenyans were very happy with their own way of doing things. It worked out well for them, and it was very pleasant. They actually never did much of anything, so nothing got screwed up by ignorant and misguided politicians. I asked one of the top people "how many bills did you pass on average in a typical year." There was a long silence. Then he said, "We passed one last year. It was about grain imports."

Once I was through with the arduous part of my assignment, which took about three hours, I was off to see the country—the Riff Valley, the wildlife, and all the exciting things I had read about as a kid in my parents' 20-year-old National Geographic magazines, which were now 50 years old. They still lived in my imagination.

I got driven around in an embassy vehicle by a chauffeur. I noticed that it was very heavy, a huge Ford SUV. I asked the chauffeur, "Why is this car so big and heavy?" "It's all the bulletproofing," he said. That sobered me up a bit. "Things must be more dangerous than I thought around here if they need to transport me around in a bulletproof car," I mused.

Unfortunately, the logistics got screwed up, Africa style, and I never got to a game refuge. My trip to the Riff Valley was just a quick drive out and back, punctuated by a "typical Kenyan lunch" consisting allegedly of roasted crocodile and other wild animals. I ate it but it didn't taste like much to me. They burned it to pieces on a big open fire. It tasted mostly like very tough smoke.

I did have time to visit some friends who lived in Nairobi, Cary Raditz and his wife Ann. Cary was famous in America as the subject of a hit song by Joni Mitchell, an old friend of his, but here in Kenya, he was just hanging out. Ann had a big job, however, in a large nonprofit organization, so they lived in a nice suburban house and had a servant or two looking after them.

Things got a little dicey at Cary and Ann's place. For some reason, I took my wallet and passport out and put them on a small table on their porch. We went inside, had a meal and a great time reminiscing about old times. When it came time to leave, I went to get my wallet and passport. Both were gone. This was a little worrisome.

Hours passed as we searched everywhere. Suddenly, the servant had an idea. He said, "That dog of Cary's has been digging in the yard all day. Maybe he took the stuff." We went out to look at the dog's accomplishments and, in one spot under a bush, something suspicious was poking out. It was my passport. The wallet was there too. The dog adopted that typical guilty "hang dog" look as he was scolded.

If not for that alert servant, I might still be in Kenya, living on burnt crocodile.

7

KAYAKING ADVENTURES–AND MISADVENTURES

FREE FALLING: NO MISTAKES ALLOWED

Some say that fear is what makes you sane. I have always felt an unusual alertness in dangerous situations, but I have never felt quite enough fear to become truly sane.

Beginning in my twenties, and lasting well into middle age, I became obsessed with kayaking. I don't mean floating around on a lake. It had to be whitewater, and the steeper and more challenging it was, the better I liked it.

Kayaking is a gravity sport. Gravity is your partner when you begin to lose altitude on a whitewater river. It might be just a little altitude loss, as in class I or II whitewater, or a big altitude loss in the case of class V water. Beyond that is the even bigger, sudden loss of altitude in free-falling off a big waterfall—fast and dramatic.

I was never a highly skilled whitewater kayaker, but I loved the sport and the whitewater rivers I was lucky to experience: the Gauley, New, Tygart, Cheat, and Blackwater in West Virginia; the Upper Youghiogheny in Maryland; the Black and Moose in New York; the Kennebec in Maine; the North Fork of the Payette in Idaho; the Tuolumne in California; the Bio Bio and Futaleufu in Chile; and dozens of others. Each river was a treasure. I measured my life by how many whitewater treasures I could collect.

Of course, this obsession had some major consequences. It ruined my marriage, leading to an ugly divorce. Not only that, but I was always paddling "over my head," meaning that I was never good enough to legitimately and comfortably navigate the rapids I was taking on. That, of course, added to the excitement.

Sometimes the rush was overwhelming. Like the first time I ever ran the Great Falls of the Potomac River, just outside of Washington, D.C. In this place, no mistakes are allowed. One wrong move at the wrong place, and you are going to go bye-bye.

I was familiar in the abstract with Great Falls. I had been kayak surfing and playing in the water below the falls for years before I had the guts—or stupidity—to try to actually run the falls. My friend Ricky Rodriguez had been running the Virginia side of the falls for some time. He talked me into it and showed me the route.

At that time, almost no one was running the falls. You could count the people who had done it on one hand. It's a different story now.

To say I was intimidated was an understatement. But I could not resist. My first run down the Virginia side of Great Falls was a rush like nothing else. There are three separate drops, ending in a vertical waterfall. Any screw-ups in the first two drops and you are toast—because the top of the final drop is no place to be swimming. I aced the first drop, slowed down and took aim at the pillow of water piling up against the boulder of the second drop, and burrowed right into it.

"Yikes!" I thought, "This is a bold move right above a big waterfall." But the pillow was soft and spun my boat right out to a good spot for taking the bottom drop on the left side, which in those days was considered to be the only runnable side. Nowadays, at higher water levels, paddlers can also take the right side.

When you hit the foam at the bottom of Great Falls for the first time, the only thing you can do to express your immense joy (and relief) is shout and throw your paddle as high as you can. Of course, after a couple of dozen runs, it gets to be not such a big thrill, but it is still always exciting.

❖ I Should Have Been More Careful ❖ 93

The author kayaking below Great Falls

After learning the Virginia side, I moved over to the Maryland side, which is potentially more dangerous. That is where most of the drownings have occurred. (There is also the Middle Route; Ricky also taught me that one. I ran it about five or six times, but never liked my chances there. At least one kayaker has died there in recent years.)

On the Maryland side, there is a notoriously bad spot about halfway down where boats and bodies can be entrapped. At least one kayaker has drowned there. I witnessed an amazing rescue at that spot by a well-known local paddler, Tom McEwan.

At the time, I was paddling behind Tom, and another friend of Tom's was behind me. Next to the dangerous spot, about halfway through the rapids, Tom pulled over into a tiny quiet spot and got out of his boat. Although I did not know why, I followed suit, because I knew Tom was an awesome paddler—as well as the first person to ever run Great Falls. I was not about to question what he was doing.

As we stood on the rock next to the second part of the drop, the third boater came down. He was too far right. Big mistake. The worst kind of mistake. He got nailed by the entrapment hole.

I have never seen anyone get into his boat and paddle out into a river quicker than Tom did that day. Within seconds, he was out next to the hole, trying to get a grip on the boat, which was circulating in the hole. The paddler was still in the boat, but had lost his paddle and was struggling. Tom pulled that boat out with the paddler still in it, while I looked on from about eight feet away, standing there with my mouth wide open in amazement. Close call. Dumb luck—or astounding skill on Tom's part? As far as I was concerned, Tom could do no wrong.

My own biggest blunder at Great Falls was on a run down the channel called the Fish Ladder, located on the far Maryland side of the falls. It is a narrow run through a series of slides with fast-moving water. Under the slides are chunks of concrete and rebar, which would grind you to hamburger meat if you ever tipped over. That aspect of the run always gives the Fish Ladder an edge.

That day, I was paddling with a friend, Rainey Hoffman, who had run the Fish Ladder a few times. Although I had run it previously without incident, Rainey was offering me some hints and guidance.

We pulled out into an eddy above the final drop, and paused. Rainey said, "You can go left or right on this final drop, but don't go down the middle." Of course, I pulled out of the eddy and went right down the middle.

Big mistake.

"BAM!" I smashed hard into a submerged rock at the bottom and got pushed back into the hole upstream of it. Pounding against the rock and getting thrown all over the place, I was experiencing the epitome of what kayakers call getting "hammered," getting "trashed," or getting "beatered." Other names have also evolved for what is an extremely tumultuous experience. Finally, I exited the boat—another bad move.

Just below the final drop is an area with swirling, whirlpool-like, vertical currents that pull you down and keep you down. This is where numerous drownings take place on the Potomac, especially among would-be swimmers. And there I was. But, unlike the swimmers, and the anglers and others who fall in accidentally, I was wearing a good life jacket. Eventually I surfaced downstream, gasping for air, and floated around the corner, to a place known as S Turn.

When my head popped up, I saw Rainey way upstream looking for me. My boat was floating away, together with my paddle and everything that had been in the boat. But, as they say, all's well that ends well. I had lucked out, as I have done so many times during my kayaking adventures—and misadventures.

THE LAST STEAK

When I started writing about kayaking for this book, I called up my friend and kayaking buddy, Henry LaBalme. Henry now lives in Connecticut with a wife and two young daughters—a radically different life from the one he led when we kayaked and partied together on the wildest whitewater rivers we could find, anywhere in the world. I asked Henry, "What do you remember about that crazy kayaking trip we took down the notorious Futaleufu River in Chile many years ago?" Henry instantly replied: "The main thing I remember is that you ate my steak."

Henry does not have the best memory. I do not recall eating Henry's steak as he alleged.

But it could have happened. We were camping next to the river with some raft guides from California. The guides had agreed to help us with transportation and food in the remote high mountain region of Patagonia through which the Futaleufu runs. It is entirely possible that the raft boys came up with some steaks for dinner. California raft guides always seemed to eat well in the wilderness. Who knows?

The alleged incident supposedly took place the day that Henry and I got separated on the river, and he disappeared. I probably thought that Henry, if he had drowned, would not have wanted a good juicy steak to go to waste or be eaten by some undeserving low-life raft guide who might be hanging around the camping spot. So, if there was an extra steak at the camp that night, I probably did eat it.

A more pertinent question is: "Where was Henry when I was supposedly chowing down on his steak?"

The Futaleufu River originates in the high mountains of Argentina and then flows through the Chilean part of Northern Patagonia, a remote and spectacularly beautiful area.

Gigantic Andean condors, with wing spans of over 10 feet, could sometimes be seen coasting high in the sky over the river. Although they mostly feed on sheep and cows, on that day Henry probably thought they were waiting to feed on him.

That day, Henry and I had been paddling our kayaks alone through some daunting rapids, many miles upstream of where we had camped. Henry flipped in a tough spot, failed a couple of attempts to roll the kayak back up, and ultimately exited his boat. I saw him climb safely ashore. I went after the boat. It took a while to capture the boat, and there was no way to paddle or bushwhack back upriver to get to Henry. So I chased the boat downstream to the camp, several miles away.

I have always wanted Henry to tell me what he had been doing in the brush and woods after exiting his kayak. I never knew how he made his way back to camp while I was, apparently, eating his steak. He didn't appear until the wee hours of the next morning, and he has never filled me in on the rest of the story about his lonely night in the woods, hiding from condors and other wild creatures.

The excitement had started long before that day. In fact, our flights down to the Futaleufu had been almost as exciting as our later adventures on the river. It's not easy to get to the Futaleufu, or anywhere else in Patagonia. The only road south, the Carreterra Austral, was seldom open in those days because of landslides in the steep terrain. Landslides were so frequent that it just was not worth the trouble to maintain the little-travelled road. In this part of Chile, the Andes slope straight down to the Pacific Ocean, creating an awesome landscape of steep mountainsides ending in a turbulent sea. A difficult area to get into and get around in.

Apart from the Carreterra Austral, the only ways to get there from Santiago were to either take a ferry to the remote island of Chiloé, bypassing the part of the coastline with all the landslides, or fly in on a small plane. We flew in—first on a plane from Santiago to Puerto

Montt, and then on a much smaller plane to an airstrip in Chaiten near the river. Landing a plane in those mountain valleys was nerve-wracking. Plane wrecks litter the coastline.

Once you finally make it to the area of the Futaleufu River, there is only a small village surrounded by large empty ranches and vast areas of immense old-growth forests. It was astounding scenery, but the attraction for us was the river. It was known to have some of the best whitewater on the planet.

Henry and I had long wanted to go there, and we had found a small California raft company willing to help with the kayaks and other logistics. For a fee, of course. We knew it could be the adventure of a lifetime.

Unfortunately, we had not fully considered the fact that this magnificent river contained rapids of a magnitude that we had never experienced. Everything on the river had been run at least once or twice by highly skilled paddlers, and two rafting outfits were taking a few brave passengers down the lower, milder portions of the river. But the upper sections were for experts only.

We were not world-class experts. We were at best mediocre kayakers. Somehow we decided that we could probably pull it off. Looking back, I realize that was not a wise decision: we were in way over our heads. The fact that we each made it out of there in one piece is pure, dumb luck.

The Futaleufu is famous for its challenging whitewater, remoteness, and pristine beauty. While kayaking, we had the river to ourselves, except for two tiny rafting encampments with very few customers about halfway down. The road was not always alongside the river because so much of the upper part of the river was in a steep-walled canyon.

"Challenging" is too weak a description for that upper whitewater section, known as the "Inferno Canyon." After seeing this section, I renamed it the "Infernal Canyon." There was nothing hot about it, but it was definitely troublesome.

The walls of the canyon at the beginning and for five miles

downstream were vertical. Not climbable for normal people without climbing gear. It was going to be a one-way trip: downriver only, with no exit. No mistakes allowed.

When Henry and I stood on the small rock ledge on the left side of the river at the beginning of this upper section, looking down at the horrendous maelstrom ahead, listening to the roar of turbulent water, we both had second thoughts: "What the hell have we gotten ourselves into?" Five miles of extreme class V and VI whitewater with no chance of looking anything over ahead of time, walking around anything, or taking out anywhere. Whew! Talk about tightening of the sphincter muscles.

There was zero possibility of scouting the section of the river we were heading into, as whitewater kayakers like to do before getting in their boats. Tall cliffs on both sides made climbing up to look around impossible. The canyon took a sharp bend to the right almost immediately. Thus the visible horizon dropped away less than 100 feet from our starting point at the top of the canyon. We knew it was going to be steep. We would be paddling blind, determining our next moves instantaneously, from the top of big waves. Anything beyond the horizon line was going to be a mystery, requiring instant reactions every moment, with no let up.

I felt a strange mix of excitement mixed with unusual alertness. We knew we had to focus and be deadly accurate with every paddle stroke. Yet we were also fueled by the anticipation of what would be the ultimate kayaking experience for both of us.

Earlier in the day we had acquired a so-called "guide" who claimed to be familiar with the required route through the long complex maze of whitewater in this section of the river. His instructions to us were simple: "Follow me. Don't deviate at all, anywhere, if you want to live through this!" That sounded promising until he took off downstream and entered the first rapid. All we could see of him was his boat flipping end-over-end repeatedly in what must have been a large hole, a spot where the water drops over a ledge and turns into furious chaos. He was getting trashed.

"Hammered" is the word kayakers use. Finally, he disappeared altogether. We never saw him again that day.

Henry looked at me with wide eyes and a nervous smile. I looked back and blurted out: "I am not going where he went!" "Me neither," echoed Henry. We stood there for a while longer, grinding our teeth to powder. There was no turning back and no way out. We looked at the fast-flowing water behind us. No going back there. We looked up at the sky above vertical canyon walls. No going up there either. Slowly and carefully we climbed into our kayaks, adjusted our spray skirts. I took a deep breath and slid into the current. I went left and Henry went right. We were both avoiding the route our skillful guide had chosen.

I made it into a tiny rollicking boil, somewhat resembling a temporary eddy. It was next to the canyon wall where I could cling momentarily with one hand to the rocks, as I bounced around apprehensively, surveying the exploding white foam downstream. It looked horrible. Confused froth and huge boulders everywhere. The river dropped down over the horizon quickly. All I could see on the banks below were a few tree tops. It was going to be steep and intense.

I realized I was probably on the wrong side of the river. There was no pathway ahead on my side, only a big jumbled sieve. Having no other choice, I took off and went hell-bent for leather for the other side of the river, where I hoped I would find a clean line and maybe even find Henry or our guide. But there was no clean line; it was just a wild lonely ride downstream for at least a mile. Rocks and huge turbulent waves and whirlpools everywhere. I focused on every stroke, constantly searching for a clean line through a huge pile of exploding water. The clean line moved around in one place, then it was somewhere else.

It was intimidating but, at the same time, exhilarating.

I finally hooked up with Henry again, and we continued. He was pale as a ghost. The river's force and intensity gradually lightened up a bit, though not by much. At some point Henry flipped in a big messy pile of steep foaming whitewater, parting company with his boat. That was when I went desperately chasing after the boat, leaving Henry to fend for himself, both for his survival and for his evening meal.

The Futaleufu contained dozens of terrifying rapids with names such as Mundaca, Casa de Piedra, Terminator, Khyber Pass, and Himalayas. In the following days, we encountered two huge ones that deserve special mention: Zeta and Throne Room. Together they constitute one of the largest and most complicated series of rapids I have seen on any river. We approached each one with trepidation and quickly realized that fully running either rapid was way beyond our ability. Could mean death. But both rapids could be partly bypassed on land! So we opted to carry our boats over the rocks on shore around the most dangerous parts.

We had come a long way to run famous rapids like Zeta and Throne Room. But by the time we got to them, we had acknowledged that at least some parts of the Futaleufu were just too hazardous for us. The next week, just after we left Patagonia, a skilled kayaker and raft guide, who had been staying at one of our camps, took on Zeta in his kayak and didn't make it. Zeta claimed his life.

Henry and I parted company in Patagonia after running every inch of the Futaleufu that we thought we could run without killing ourselves. He went on up the Chilean coast to meet Doug Tompkins, a wealthy San Francisco philanthropist who had a hideaway in the woods. Henry was trying to hit Tompkins up for funding for one of Henry's pie-in-the-sky nonprofit schemes. Something about television.

I took off hitchhiking across the top of the Southern Andes, on a lonely road into Argentina. It was several days before the first vehicle came by. That trip was another adventure, but it was mild fare after our adrenaline-soaked runs down the Futaleufu.

The bottom line is that I probably owe Henry LaBalme a steak. I plan to buy him one the next time he comes to town.

FEAR CAN BE YOUR FRIEND: A SHORT ESSAY

It is said that before entering the sea
a river trembles with fear....

The river needs to take the risk
of entering the ocean
because only then will fear disappear,
because that's where the river will know
it's not about disappearing into the ocean,
but of becoming the ocean.

-Khalil Gibran, "Fear"

The question is: why do people like to scare the crap out of themselves? I cannot speak for others, but I voluntarily experienced a lot of fear when I was younger, kayaking whitewater rivers all over the world. Fear of a tremendous whitewater monster rapid that you are about to kayak through strikes suddenly. It is cold, physical, and immediate. Then suddenly it's gone, replaced by a streaming flow of something else.

The odd thing is that I never experienced the fear ahead of time, when I could have planned to avoid the situation entirely. "No big deal," I always thought. Then, later, when the moment of truth arrived, fear struck. It was not debilitating, however. You can use your fear. You can ride it like a wild horse. You can transform it into intense focus, allowing you to avoid death and disaster.

Getting psyched to run a rapid

A famous kayaker, Doug Ammons, has written eloquently about how he kayaks the most intense and dangerous whitewater on the planet experiencing no fear at all, only a Zen-like calm.[15] Then there was "Fearless Fred," another kayaker who feared nothing ever. I once took a ride with him on a road beside the river. He drove fast, wrecked the car into a telephone pole on a curve, backed up, cursed, and hit the pedal again. I later heard that he quit kayaking and bought a small airplane.

Unlike those two, I do experience fear, at least initially. I found that fear has its uses. Without fear, I would have no special awareness. Without that jolt, I would never enjoy the experience of kayaking through a ridiculously steep, fast drop in a lethal churning maelstrom of whitewater.

At the top of a terrifying descent over a huge rapid or waterfall, a kind of quiet awareness suddenly ambushes me, wrapping me in its embrace—as though an alien force has taken over my body and mind. The focus becomes FIGHT OR FLIGHT. First I scan the surroundings for an escape, thinking: "How do I get out of this predicament?"

If flight is not possible, then I wonder: "HOW DID I GET MYSELF INTO THIS STUPID PREDICAMENT?!" And: "Why didn't I think about this before I got this deep in?"

---

[15] Doug Ammons, *Whitewater Philosophy* (Water Nymph Press, 2009).

Next, things come quickly into focus. Left brain says to right brain: "Don't panic here. You will get wasted if you panic. Better recheck the equipment. Calm down!"

Right brain says back: "OK. OK. OK. Just look this monster over one more time. There MUST be a way through this mess. Maybe some way to sneak down the side?"

"Damn! No sneaking through this monster anywhere."

"Well. I guess that's why it's rated a class V rapid."

"There must be a line through this somewhere. Maybe I could start left, slip past the small hole at top center left, then the big one just below in the center. But don't get caught in the nasty rock on the left. Then immediately charge hard right fighting through the huge curlers to reach a spot near the canyon wall. Maybe a micro eddy will be there to get my bearings and see what's next. What is causing those huge exploding waves and boils?"

"It's all hidden below the horizon. Miles to go steeply downhill through who knows what."

"Yikes! What a mess!"

"Stay cool. This must be doable. Only three people have died here recently. Others made it through. Maybe the water level was higher? Maybe it was lower? Maybe it was dark and they couldn't see what they were getting into? Who knows?"

Body, now thoroughly detached from the mental turmoil, slips on autopilot into the familiar kayak seat.

Left brain warns: "Better get your spray skirt on good and tight. If it blows, you are history."

The initial jitters don't go away completely until the boat plunges irreversibly into the froth, picking up speed. Then jitters are suddenly and completely gone, replaced with intense focus.

"HOLY COW! This stuff is beyond belief."

I am swallowed up by massive chaotic waves, gigantic slabs of confused whitewater. I flip over. Then roll up. Then again. I back ender and flip a third time. Roll up a third time.

"This is wild! Horrendous…but where did fear go?"

No room for fear. Too much else going on. And actually, it's amazing fun.[16]

DISASTER AVERTED AT THE GAULEY FEST

It was a dark and stormy night.

Maybe not all that dark, but it WAS raining cats and dogs. Cars were stuck in the mud all over the place. A small bunch of kayakers in a rented field in southern West Virginia were trying to jump-start a festival for whitewater boaters.

There was a big dam on the Gauley River, run by the U.S. Army Corps of Engineers. Below that dam was a rocky gorge with a little water trickling down through it. Nothing special. But when the Corps released water from the dam, all of Summerville Lake began to flow into that gorge. It was one of the best whitewater runs in the entire United States. Maybe in the world.

The releases from Summerville Lake through the dam were made in the fall of each year to allow the lake to fill up again over the winter and spring, controlling flooding downstream. Rafters and kayakers

---

[16] What is going on is not technically an adrenaline rush. It's more of a "flow" state of mind. According to Boyd Ruppelt, an expert kayaker and skydiver on the Whitewater Team at Jackson Kayak: "Adrenaline makes things happen too fast, causes mistakes, and leaves you feeling exhausted and pumped with the stress hormone, cortisol. Adrenaline makes it harder to think, harder to make decisions, harder to perform, and therefor [sic] harder to survive. Flow does something different. Flow makes things slow down, improves your performance, promotes clear and crisp thinking, and leaves you feeling balanced and energized. . . . It inhibits the cortisol." In the flow state, he says, "you feel super human, time distorts and things slow down. . . . Skill takes over and the best of you comes out. That's flow, not adrenaline." Facebook, September 7, 2022, https://www.facebook.com/Boyd.Ruppelt.Jr/posts/pfbid02NAP3EMFAPtTUgL3eEXk93cb4Yvqy2RJ4yCDtjpzme9KD7dAVjGw2dDGxjtNgqDMyl.

Ruppelt also has an awesome video on the Jackson Kayak website about how to manage fear in high-risk situations. "Dealing With Fear," accessed December 30, 2022, https://hub.jacksonkayak.com/2022/11/dealing-with-fear-2/.

from all over the eastern U.S. and beyond would show up to take advantage of the fabulous whitewater produced on the Gauley by the scheduled releases.

At that time, a few kayakers, mostly from the east coast, were beginning to worry about the loss of the whitewater rivers they loved. There were multiple problems. Many older, hydroelectric-power dams, mostly in New York and New England, were up for relicensing by the Federal Energy Regulatory Commission. Other dams, like the one on the Gauley, were not yet operating for hydropower but were the target of efforts to install generating turbines, which would end the dam releases needed for whitewater rafting and kayaking. A third category of rivers were not yet dammed but were being eyed with relish by power companies.

Another emerging problem was neighboring landowners and local authorities blocking access to the rivers.

A lot of great whitewater paddling opportunities were on the chopping block. These observant kayakers worried that the magnificent river resources they loved were going to be lost to recreational paddlers.

Some of those kayakers were members of a tiny, obscure organization, the American Whitewater Affiliation (AWA), which published a journal that contained stories of thrilling whitewater runs around the country. The organization had no other mission—especially not big-ticket river-conservation challenges.

A small but intrepid group of AWA members—including Pete Skinner and Chris Kroll of New York, and me in Washington, D.C.—saw an opportunity to transform the AWA into a national organization with the mission of protecting and preserving whitewater in America. We wanted to make life difficult for the power developers and dam builders.

Our initial problems were money and membership. AWA had little of either.

Pete Skinner—a mercurial, persistent spark plug working as an environmental engineer—flew to California to try to raise some cash. After several misfires with environmental philanthropists in San Francisco, he went after Yvon Chouinard, the eccentric founder and owner of Patagonia. Pete tracked down Chouinard out back of his factory and store in Ventura, picking up garbage. Pete, a persuasive fast talker, swiftly filled Chouinard in on the situation. Chouinard replied, "How much do you need?" Caught off guard for the first time in his life, Pete replied, "$10,000." A few minutes later he realized he should have said "$100,000," because Chouinard immediately said "done" and invited Pete over for dinner.

That first grant got AWA going. With those initial funds, we launched our effort to protect whitewater resources, starting with those in New York. However, we knew we would need to find a continuous infusion of cash to wage a nationwide war with big, rich electric power companies and the Corps of Engineers.

We put our heads together and realized that whitewater enthusiasts had one large national gathering: the hundreds of kayakers and rafters that showed up at the Gauley River in West Virginia every fall. So, we mused, why not have a big festival there, and try to make a little money out of their visits, while promoting AWA? The Gauley River Festival, now a famous annual event attended by thousands, grew out of those daydreams.

The Friends of the Gauley River, a small local group, was already holding a small fundraiser at the dam site every year, in an effort to save the Gauley releases. AWA members Steve Taylor, Charlie Walbridge, and I were working with that group. After some deliberating, a deal was struck: the AWA would take over the small fundraising event and promote it as a major national effort to save the nation's rivers— starting with the Gauley and the Black and Moose Rivers in New York.

Thus, AWA cut its teeth on a small festival in a field near the Summerville Dam, held jointly with the Friends of the Gauley.

That first festival was not much of a money maker. For the second festival, a small group of AWA members got to work on finding more space, entertainment, vendors, and volunteers. A band and a wrestling bear were booked to provide entertainment. My friends and

AWA compatriots, Risa Shimoda, Jack Hession, and others served barbecued chicken and corn on the cob for the hungry mob.

The bear never showed up. (It was stolen by a raft outfitter who offered to pay the bear's owner more for a party of his own elsewhere.) And it rained like hell most of the evening. Even with those setbacks, however, the event was a raging success in terms of the good times people had, the kegs consumed, and the thousands of greenbacks collected at the gate, for raffle tickets and for the dinner.

Overall, the festival was going well. Then, disaster struck. Sometimes, one little incident changes history. In this case, alcohol was involved.

First, the Perception Kayak Company gave me an award for river conservation, and I saw an opportunity to take over the stage with my rant about the "god-damn fucking hydropower dams." I had consumed a vast quantity of alcohol, so I suspect that I raved on incoherently for a while. That could explain why the audience was throwing beer cans at me. Ultimately, I staggered off the stage into the mud.

Then, the two most inebriated AWA leaders—Chris and I—were entrusted with the money. We stuck it in a bag and continued our attempt to drink each other under the table.

Ultimately, we both passed out on the stage, drunk as skunks, lying in rain and mud. When we awoke, the bag, with thousands of dollars in it, was nowhere to be found.

Both of us had legendary hangovers. We sat in the mud in silent misery. We had totally screwed up.

As the sun arose, Paul Breuer, an outfitter who was working with AWA on the effort to protect the Gauley flows, drove by the two sad-looking drunkards in his truck. Looking at our miserable expressions, he asked, "What's up, guys? Missing something?"

We started to explain our misfortune. Then Paul raised an ammo box up from his truck seat.

Paul had seen us passed out, clutching a bag, and easily figured out what was going on. He lifted the money and stashed it in his safe back at his rafting headquarters until more sober individuals could be found to protect it.

At least that's the way I remember the incident. Paul was the unsung hero, the *deus ex machina*, of the second AWA Gauley Fest. Those two clowns who passed out clutching the money would prefer to forget the whole incident. Their memories are suspect.

Despite the drunken debacle, the AWA survived and flourished, the Gauley Fest grew beyond anyone's imagination, and, best of all, the Gauley and other whitewater rivers have been protected from the depredation of power companies and other environmental villains. The Gauley River gorge is now a National Recreation Area. The Black and Moose Rivers are hosting thousands of rafters and kayakers every year.

PIGS WITH HORNS

It was my third night camping out in southern Chile in the high Andes. As I drifted off to sleep, the Southern Cross lit up the cloudless sky. I began to dream of the steep Andean rivers with 30-foot waterfalls, one right after another, some of the most magical whitewater anywhere in the world for whitewater kayakers.

Suddenly, I was startled by a gruff huffing outside my tent. I heard guttural noises. Something knocked a pot off the rocks near the campfire embers. Drowsily I forced open my eyes and peeked out from my raggedy little tent. I spotted a hulking form in the moonlight. It looked like a very large pig. But this was no normal pig. It had large pointy things protruding ominously from its head.

"Jeez," I thought to myself, "Do the pigs down here have antlers? I could get gored to death by a porker and my family would never know how I died."

Then the realization set in: this could be even worse than my last campsite on the Rio Maipo, where a nest of hairy baseball-sized spiders attempted to evict us from the area.

After having downed a bottle of cheap (I am talking less than

$1 U.S.) Chilean wine, and a few glasses of the local 150 proof stuff called "pisco," before bedtime, I did not feel up to doing battle with a horned pig. On the other hand, this malevolent and peculiar creature was busy raiding our precious food stash.

"If that bastard gets our peanut butter," I thought, "this trip is over. No way can American kayakers survive three and a half more weeks in the high Andes without peanut butter." (They don't sell peanut butter in Chile. That fact alone makes you crave it, even if you never liked it at home.)

Summoning what little energy I had in the tank, I wearily staggered out of the tent and lurched unsteadily toward the monster.

"This could be an uneven match," I realized. "Those horns are huge and ugly."

I needed a weapon. I scanned the area for something. Anything. Finding a good-sized rock, I cranked up my battle cry (actually more of a drunken squawk) and staggered toward the creature. He gave me a sullen look until I heaved the rock. It caught him between the eyes. He uttered a squeal of indignation and sauntered off into the darkness.

This was not the first time I had encountered trouble in Chile. The country is a paradise for American kayakers, but there are a few issues. Besides the peculiar pigs, there are huge hairy spiders, and the fabled cooliewatcha. I have no idea how that name is spelled in English, but they are unmistakable when they arrive. The cooliewatcha is a huge flying insect, somewhat like an obese black fly, with a voracious appetite for human flesh. They hang out in large numbers in Chile's Lake District. On rivers they fly in large flocks. I was breakfast, lunch, and dinner for cooliewatcha gangs more than once.

As much as I loved kayaking the magnificent Chilean rivers, what I remember most is choking on dust as we hiked up twisty mountain roads, chasing the pigs with horns, swatting cooliewatchas, and smashing spiders. Another strange incident stands out, even among these hazards. Where else could you meet up, close and personal, with the goon squad of a real live South American dictator, and survive?

That day, I was boating down the Maipo River, just upstream

of a rapid known as "Pinochet's Hole," with two other kayakers. Generalissimo Pinochet had, until recently, been the all-powerful dictator of Chile. In some kind of political deal orchestrated most likely by the American CIA, Pinochet had been retired, and a democratic government replaced him for the first time in decades. The deal allowed Pinochet to retire to some of his many luxurious residences around the country and live the good life, no matter how many of his opponents had disappeared or fallen out of helicopters.

Unknown to us, Pinochet's Hole marked the boundary of the generalissimo's ranch. Just before arriving at the hole, we had an incident in which we lost some vital equipment. We were forced to climb out of the river canyon on foot. We were trespassing, although we did not know that at the time. The generalissimo's hacienda was in sight as we headed out on foot, carrying our kayaks toward where we thought we could find a road.

Suddenly, a large group of soldiers appeared out of a trench surrounding the hacienda. We had surprised them by coming from the river side. They were not happy. They had large assault weapons. They yelled demands at us in Spanish, which we failed to comprehend. The situation was tense until the soldiers deduced from our confused mumblings in bastardized Spanish that we were innocent lost *norteamericanos* who had stumbled unwittingly into a dangerous situation.

They escorted us out the front gate. Crisis averted.

We never saw Pinochet. Maybe he was at another of his many mansions that day.

Later on during this Chilean Adventure, I discovered, under closer examination, that the horns on the pig were not real ones. They were wooden contraptions that Chilean farmers strapped onto the heads of their pigs to prevent them from squeezing under the fences and escaping. Unbeknownst to us, the campsite we selected the night we were attacked by the pig was INSIDE a farmer's pig pen. Our situational awareness on that trip was not the best.

8

WE BE SAILIN', MON

WE WERE DAMN LUCKY

Nostalgia ain't what it used to be.
—Peter De Vries, *The Tents of Wickedness*, 1959

It was morning when I crawled up on the sandy beach, exhausted and nearly naked. There was a rope around my waist. My dad was tied to the other end, about 10 feet away, and he was also scrambling onto the beach. The sun was just coming up.

We spit sand out of our mouths. Huge waves were breaking over us, left over from a massive storm the night before. Our life jackets were shredded, and Dad was bleeding a little from his head and back.

Dad said to me, "Son. We were damn lucky." I thought he was nuts. We had shipwrecked! He had lost everything: his boat, which he lived on, and all his stuff, including all his valuables.

"Lucky?" I thought to myself. "How was that lucky?"

Just a few hours earlier we had been standing on the stern of my dad's classic old wooden sailboat, *Windward*, clinging to whatever we could as the boat, half filled with water, wallowed in gigantic breaking waves. Surrounding us was the wildest ocean I have ever seen. Wind screaming like a banshee, blowing the tops off waves. The sea churning violently in all directions. Ocean spray everywhere.

We were breathing salt water in with every breath we took. Visibility was near zero because it was pitch dark, except during lightning strikes. During those brief moments, the scene around me was so far beyond terrifying that I did not know what to think or feel.

Anyone who has been at sea in a bad storm will know what I mean when I say that the power of the ocean and wind is unimaginable. As one of the survivors of the Pride of Baltimore disaster said, "When you go out to sea, it's a big place out there and the sea has all the power."

At the time of the wreck, we didn't know where we were, just that we were out to sea and it was a big, unpleasant place to be. The sea had all the power.

In my decades-long sailing career, I have endured an inordinate number of unfortunate seafaring experiences. But nothing else has been as dramatic and unfortunate as the loss of my dad's boat, *Windward*. I was only 29 years old, and my dad was in his sixties, retired, divorced, and still strong and healthy.

Windward was an attractive, sturdy, 40-year-old wooden sloop, designed by Sparkman and Stevens in their New York City headquarters. While she was a seaworthy boat, she was not well set up for long ocean passages. She was just 30 feet long—big enough to carry a small dinghy on deck, but not big enough for both a dinghy and an inflatable life raft. My dad chose to carry the dinghy because he did mostly inland sailing, with only short, one-day offshore hops in the ocean. He lived on the boat year-round, moving up and down the coast following the weather as it warmed up or cooled off.

Although my dad sailed the boat alone most of the time, my two brothers, plus many of our friends, girlfriends, and wives, sailed with him on *Windward* for a while every year as he cruised up and down the coast.

On the fateful occasion that ended our pleasant adventures on that boat, I was alone with Dad, taking Christmas leave from my office job. On the morning of December 22, 1971, we motored out through the Cape Canaveral inlet into the big blue peaceful ocean, headed for south Florida. We hoped to end up in the Florida Keys, several days away. With two aboard, we could sail day and night by taking turns being on watch and sleeping. Our back-up plan if the weather turned bad was to go back in at Fort Pierce, a large inlet with good ocean access just 70 nautical miles (about 80 statute miles) to the south of Cape Canaveral. The weather report was nothing to stress about. No bad weather predicted.

We left at sunrise, hoping to pass the Fort Pierce inlet before nightfall and continue south through the night and the next day.

The sail plan was to stay inside of the powerful north-flowing Gulf Stream, but far enough away from shore to avoid shallow offshore sand banks. The Gulf Stream can be a sailor's nightmare. It is a powerful warm-water river flowing north through the cold Atlantic seas. If the wind is blowing south (a "northerly"), the wind against current creates an ugly mess of steep confused waves. By staying closer to shore, however, you can sail south on a northerly breeze without facing the Gulf Stream waves. But staying closer to shore has its own problems, as we learned the hard way.

Our problems started almost immediately beyond Cape Canaveral. The engine was acting up. Finally it uttered a death rattle and stopped completely. I asked, "What just happened?" Dad said, "It sometimes dies when bigger ocean waves stir up the fuel. Water condenses inside the fuel tank walls. The violent motion of ocean waves sloshes fuel around the tank, causing water to mix with the fuel, fouling it."

I was not crazy about losing the engine, but it was not fatal to our trip because we were sailing south with a good breeze behind us. On the other hand, getting into an inlet later, anywhere on the Florida Coast, would be nearly impossible if we could not get the engine going. I thought to myself, "We will make it somehow." The sailing was good, and for a while I put the inlet issue out of my mind.

Then, around noon, the radio failed for no obvious reason. This denied us weather updates and contact with the Coast Guard and other boats. By this time we were too far south to change plans, and the wind was strengthening and taking us south quickly. So south we went.

I thought to myself, "We could get pretty far south under sail with these nice strong north winds we are experiencing." But the question of how we would get into an inlet under sail continued to nag at me. "How in the world could we sail into any inlet if things got rough?"

In the late afternoon, as we got closer to Fort Pierce, the weather turned weird. The sky blackened. A dangerous nor'easter was bearing down on us. We donned our life jackets and hooked ourselves onto the boat with sailors' storm harnesses.

Wind speeds rose quickly in the late afternoon. Powerful gusts screamed through the boat's rigging, making the boat hard to steer. Waves grew bigger and steeper, and the tops started to break off in white foam. "Not a good sign," I thought to myself. As the storm grew, we took down our normal sails and put up as little sail as we could. A huge, unpredicted weather system was blowing us south and west very hard.

To the west was the Florida coast. It was what sailors call a "lee shore," meaning that wind and waves from offshore can push you ashore. Ashore is, paradoxically, not where you want to be. On the edge of the ocean is where ships die, on rocks and shoals in shallow water. No safe harbors were available between Cape Canaveral and Fort Pierce.

We tried to sail farther offshore, to get away from the dangerous shoreline and shallows. But the seas were shoving us around so much that the best we could do was to continue south. At least we were getting closer to Fort Pierce, and, if the storm eased up, we could have tried to get in the inlet there.

We were delusional about the possibility of entering the Fort Pierce inlet. Even in 20 knots of wind and 6-foot seas, that inlet, in fact any ocean inlet, is big trouble under sail with no engine. We were enduring more than 50 or 60 knots of howling winds, and seas that seemed three stories high. Those waves were steep—almost vertical. I thought to myself, as I looked straight up to the foaming top of a wave, "That does not look like any wave I have ever seen. It looks more like a big heavy black wall of water about to fall down and crush us!"

In those conditions, the inlet would have been filled with similar monster breaking waves, which would have thrown *Windward* like a toothpick into who-knows-what jetty or shoreline. The wooden dinghy, strapped on the deck, was already pounded into splinters. I was seasick for a while, the first and only time in my life. Puking repeatedly. Too seasick to be scared.

When facing a life-or-death situation and a lot of uncertainty, people react differently. Some are terrified. Some are paralyzed. Some shut down. I felt intensely aware. I noticed everything around me, and thought of everything and anything that could make the situation come out well. I snapped out of the seasickness, and felt like I gained enormous energy.

As darkness approached, we continued to try to get offshore as far as possible; but since we could not get the boat to go east at all, in desperation, finally, late at night, we decided to see if we could anchor. Anchoring was a last-ditch desperate move. Anchoring meant going into shallower water. Shallower water meant bigger waves, all of them breaking.

I thought to myself, "Anchoring is not going to work in this maelstrom, even if we can get the anchor down." We both knew that, but we knew had to do something to stay off the shore and try to survive.

By crawling slowly forward, clinging to the deck, I managed to get to the anchor and release it from its deck storage. I dropped it overboard. Suddenly, the boat jerked hard. It held to the anchor, on 150 feet of anchor line. It continued to hold for maybe an hour. But the boat was bucking violently and being hammered by huge breaking waves. The boat and anchor line were under incredible stress. Waves crashed down on us like giant collapsing buildings, burying the entire boat underwater like a toy. We had attached ourselves to the boat by clipping our storm harnesses onto lifelines (called "tethering") so we would not get separated from the boat. After each pounding, the boat would slowly float back up to face the next monster, and, each time, we were still aboard.

Suddenly, a gigantic wave broke through the hatch cover—a solid oak hatch cover reinforced with steel. At that point, I thought to myself: "Now we are well and truly screwed." No sailboat does well in a massive storm with an open hatch. We now had no hatch cover at all. Only splinters remained.

The boat filled up quickly with gallons and gallons of seawater flooding through the hatch. We bailed as much as we could with a bucket, but our efforts amounted to almost nothing against the huge inflow. I yelled to Dad, "We are going to sink!" He did not reply, but the expression on his face spoke volumes.

In less than 10 minutes, the boat went under again, this time for good. We stayed clipped on to the stainless steel back stay, a wire that connected the mast to the stern of the boat, until it was clear that we would only be dragged down with the boat. We unclipped when the upper deck of the boat slipped beneath the foaming seas. It was on its way to a place my dad always referred to as "Davey Jones' Locker," the bottom of the ocean.

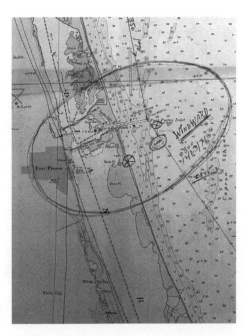

Chart showing where Windward sank

Now, we were floating in the ocean without a boat or life raft, in a raging storm, somewhere off the shore of Florida, being tossed around like ping-pong balls. Fortunately, the Florida waters were not killing cold. Our demise was going to be a slow one, I thought. Dad yelled at me over the storm noise: "Get that line floating next to you!" I clutched a floating piece of rope and tied it to my waist. He got the other end on his waist.

The rope was a good idea. We could communicate a bit over the noise of the wind and seas and not lose each other.

That is how we faced the remainder of the night. We still had life jackets on, and we were hopeful that we would eventually blow ashore instead of drifting for days in the direction of Key West or Cuba.

Hours later, the storm began to abate a little and the sun tried to come up. As I crested a monster wave, in the dim morning light, I caught a brief glimpse of something that looked to me like a tree top. I shouted, "Dad! I think I saw land!"

I will never forget his depressing admonition: "Don't kid your old man at a time like this."

I shut up about tree tops, but still I had some hope that it was not an illusion. My dad was always good company. I always enjoyed being with him. But now he was totally silent. He was exhausted, barely holding on, and bleeding from cuts he had gotten when the wire rigging that held up the mast ripped apart and whipped around the boat like a knife. I started to worry about sharks sensing his blood. I furtively looked around for shark fins. None in view. "Whew! Thank God for that at least!"

About an hour or so later, huge breaking shore surf threw us violently onto the beach, almost naked, with our life jackets in shreds. The rope tying us together had held. We untied and looked at each other in amazement.

The only thing my exhausted dad said was: "We were damn lucky."

He was dead right.

We had landed on the barrier island off the Florida coast, not far from the Fort Pierce inlet. We dragged our water-logged bodies up to a house on the shore and knocked on the door. A frightened woman peeked carefully through a crack in the door. Seeing us, she looked totally horrified. We muttered, "Our boat sank. We need help."

We were semi-nude and bedraggled. The woman said, "Stay there. I am calling the cops." We replied, "Please do. Call anyone!" We collapsed on her front porch. It was still raining hard with wind blowing like crazy, and we welcomed the feel of the steady porch under us. It was not moving like a bucking bronco. The stability made me dizzy after so much motion. It felt incredibly good.

The cops came in less than an hour and took us to the police station in Fort Pierce where, observing our shredded clothing, they gave us convict jump suits and a cell with two cots. They had no other place to take us since we did not need emergency medical treatment. Thankfully, they did not lock us in.

After hearing our harrowing story, the police called the newspaper. A reporter arrived and we gave interviews that showed up in the Fort Pierce paper the next day. The headline was deadly accurate: "Two Sailors Survive Major Storm Offshore." The article was accompanied by a picture of the two of us in prison clothes.

That was the second and last time I have been in jail in my life, and—this time—I could not have been happier about being there safe and sound.

Bits and pieces of *Windward* showed up on the beach in the following days. We collected some things, but scavengers got most of it. I still have a deck cleat from the beach debris, which I use for a door handle in my house.

Cleat from Windward

Afterwards, my dad moved onto another boat. I continued sailing another 50 years, but for a long time I avoided the ocean. It took 20 years for me to gather up the courage to go back offshore on a sailboat. And when I did, I swore that I would take with me every kind of safety gear known to man.

SAILING WITH A SCAREDY-CAT

I have had a number of sailing adventures—and misadventures—in addition to the shipwreck off the Florida coast described in the story "We Were Damn Lucky." A memorable one is the time I attempted to sail across the Atlantic Ocean from Martinique in the Caribbean to the Mediterranean, but did not make it all the way to the European mainland.

Then there is the time I was aboard a sailboat that crashed into a railroad bridge.

I have lost rudders on two occasions, once in the Atlantic, far from land.

I have endured numerous death-defying, anchor-dragging incidents, mostly in the Bahamas, and many engine failures up to and including the total loss of the engine.

I have been traumatized by sailing through all of the Windward Islands with a drunken Dutchman.

Maybe I will eventually get around to telling more of those stories.

But for now I want to tell of a sailing trip with Amber Jones. Amber and I have been partners and lovers for 20 years. During that time, I continually wanted to go sailing. Amber was never a big fan of sailing. Early in our relationship, she stayed home and continued working at her writing job with the U.S. Government, happy not to have to participate in my "idiotic and frightening" ocean adventures.

On those trips, I was usually on someone else's boat. I hired myself out as ocean-sailing crew on boats going all over the place: offshore to Maine, to Panama, around the Azores, back from Bermuda, and from the Chesapeake Bay to the Bahamas or Caribbean and back, many times. They were exceptional trips with interesting people.

Finally, Amber agreed to retire so we could take a long sailing trip together. For this, we needed our own boat. Without properly consulting Amber, I fell in love with, and bought, a 1984 30-foot O'Day sloop named *Integrity*. The owner was a Catholic priest in Annapolis. The name he had chosen, *Integrity*, was clearly inappropriate for a boat of mine. Maybe not for the priest's either, since the boat seemed a bit neglected. One of my dad's beloved boats was named *Echo*, so we changed the name of our new boat to *Echo II*. Dad's other boat was *Windward*, but I was reluctant to borrow that name since *Windward* was at the bottom of the ocean offshore of Florida. Seemed bad luck to name a boat after one you sank.

There are two ways to take a long trip on an old boat that is new to you. One is to spend several years getting the boat fixed up and in seagoing shape. Then go, if you are not too old by then. The other way is to just fill up the fuel tank with diesel and go, discovering problems en route as they arise. Of course, the latter was the clear choice for me, although Amber had reservations from the start.

To begin with, she said the boat was full of mold. I was skeptical, because I couldn't smell it. Also, Amber is a total, dyed-in-the-wool scaredy-cat. She fears just about everything. Fears getting robbed. Fears getting shot. Fears buying the wrong furniture, being late, and speaking in public. She lives in a deep black pool of fear.

While Amber is 100% scaredy-cat, she is also determined to confront and overcome her fears, one way or another. She traveled to many places alone, sometimes homesick and in tears, but determined to see the world. When she realized that her terror of public speaking was holding her back at work, she joined Toastmasters and made hundreds of speeches in public, overcoming the paralysis she started with and becoming an exceptionally good speaker.

One of Amber's biggest challenges is the fear of drowning. For her to quit her job and go sailing with me to parts unknown, on an old, poorly maintained boat, was quite a test of overcoming that fear. She figured that if she could get on the boat and go the distance, she could defeat her fear of drowning at sea.

We decided to see if we could make it to the Bahamas and cruise the Abacos, Exumas, and other beautiful island chains in that area.

Amber cleaned up some of the mold, and off we went, without even checking the oil.

Amber on Echo II in Miami, before crossing the Gulf Stream

Since the boat was new to us, we decided not to take the open ocean route from the Chesapeake Bay, but to travel down the Intracoastal Waterway (ICW) to Florida, then make the ocean crossing to the Bahamas from there. The ICW involved a lot of motoring and many possibilities for running aground, but at least there were places to stop for repairs, if needed. And oh boy, were they needed!

I joked that, during that trip, I paid the tuition for the college educations of the children of every mechanic on the ICW between Annapolis and Florida. We broke down everywhere. Our first major breakdown was in North Myrtle Beach, South Carolina. The cooling system went kaput. A week passed while we waited for Sea Pupp Boat Repairs to come up with a new water pump. The ICW breakdowns and repairs continued down through South Carolina, Georgia, and Florida. Many nice mechanics helped us out. For a price.

The author repairing the engine of Echo II

Then there were the groundings. Amber tended to get panicky about running aground, but I was accustomed to it. After all, back in the Chesapeake Bay, I had earned the title "Captain Runaground." By the time we finished the Bahamas trip, I had truly earned a promotion to Admiral.

Constantly breaking down and getting stuck on the bottom did not do much to inspire Amber's confidence in the boat, or in me as captain. Then there was the freezing cold weather we endured all the way from Maryland to northern Florida, with no heat on the boat. Some mornings, the deck was covered with ice.

What almost completely finished her off, however, was the crossing of the Gulf Stream from Miami to Bimini in the Bahamas.

The Gulf Stream can be a dangerous place. It is an open ocean crossing with a notoriously powerful northbound current. When the winds are from the north and strong, opposing the current, the Gulf Stream cannot be crossed at all in a small boat like *Echo II*. One must wait until things quiet down.

We decided to depart Florida from a place called No Name Harbor, just south of Miami. Sitting around No Name listening to the weather predictions was not helping Amber's emotional condition. Her dread index was in the red zone and bumping upward hourly.

Finally, the forecast looked doable. We pulled up the anchor in the dark and took off well before dawn, headed for the little island of Bimini. It was an 8- to 10-hour trip in our boat, and you cannot enter the Bimini harbor after dark. There are no lights or reliable markers for the harbor entrance, and the entrance has a treacherous left-hand turn that is unmarked. So we needed to leave early to get to the Bimini entrance in daylight.

Off we went about 3 am. But the forecast was wrong. The seas had got up, and the boat was thrown around like a cork in the dark. The worst problem was that, as the boat slammed into the waves, the fiberglass hull would flex ever so slightly. Since the caulking between the hull and deck had been drying out since 1984, sea water began sneaking in through that joint, mostly along the bow, right above where our sleeping area was located, in the V berth. Amber desperately tried to protect our bedding, but it was hopeless. She reported to me that water was "pouring in."

Failing to stop the leaks, and being tossed and turned like a ping-pong ball, Amber ended up down in the cabin, curled in the fetal position, sobbing. I was getting nervous myself. I told her, "I think the wise thing to do is to turn back and wait for better conditions." She replied, "I agree. And if we get back to Florida alive, I am getting off this damn boat and never getting on a boat again."

That put me in a bit of a dilemma. I did not want to lose my crew so early in the trip. So I hesitated, considered my options, and decided to continue to sail toward Bimini.

Fortunately, after several hours, conditions moderated. We made it into the Bimini harbor and docked. It was Christmas Eve.

I was putting things together on the deck when I saw Amber climbing off the boat with her bags packed, carrying all her stuff. She asked Bruce Donadt, the captain of the boat next to us, "Where is the airport?" He said, "There is no airport here." Stunned, Amber broke down in tears. Bruce offered her a Dark and Stormy, a famous sailors' rum drink, to calm her nerves. Bruce's wife Gayleen tried to convince Amber that it was not always that bad out in the big ocean. She also invited us to Christmas dinner. Amber downed the Dark and Stormy, and then a few more. Finally, she went to sleep.

I breathed a sigh of relief. Another *deus ex machina*, Gayleen, had saved me again.

Amber stayed onboard for the rest of that trip—breakdowns, leaks, and all—and for many others over the years. We drank Dark and Stormies with Bruce and Gayleen whenever we crossed paths again. She is still a scaredy-cat, but she is also now an exceptionally competent crew member.

Amber had some comments to add to this story. One of them was this: "Pope neglected to mention that he bought, from the same shifty broker that sold him the broken-down sailboat, a used inflatable dinghy for $200. The first time we tried to pump it up to row ashore in North Carolina, it was clear that it would end up on the bottom with us in it. Pope, characteristically, said 'no problem; we'll row fast.' However, my fear of drowning won the day. I made Pope stop at a West Marine shop in a coastal town so I could buy a brand new inflatable dinghy and outboard engine for $1,000. It was my money or my life."

CAPTAIN RUNAGROUND

I have run aground many times in my life, both figuratively and in actuality. I ran aground in all of my marriages and in most of my other relationships with women. It was the same with sailboats. Aground more often than not. It became so common that I was referred to by those brave warriors who foolishly went sailing with me as "Captain Runaground." Some still refer to me that way, although others who know me better have promoted me to "Admiral Runaground."

Some groundings have been no big deal, but a few were epic.

Take, for example, the time that my partner, Amber, and I were sailing in the Exumas, a beautiful chain of islands in the Bahamas. We were having a wonderful time until we decided to anchor overnight in a narrow channel inside a large, deserted cove. Shallow water on both sides of the channel. I wondered why no other boats were in there, but it looked nice, and so down went the hook.

Our anchor was a state-of-the-art Rocna, a new-generation anchor proved in testing to hold better than any of the old Danforths and CQRs. The Rocnas don't drag. So they said.

Feeling supremely confident, we set the anchor firmly and then had a nice spaghetti dinner and dozed happily off to sleep. Sometime during the night, we noticed a strange sound, a bumping and scraping noise. Then the boat began to tilt. The tide had reversed 180 degrees, and, in turning around, the anchor had failed to reset. Not only was it loose, but the anchor line had wrapped tightly around the keel. It was impossible to get the anchor up on deck.

We were aground, bumping up and down on a reef of some kind, with the tide going out and no effective anchor. If we drifted east over the reef, the next stop was Portugal. If we stayed on the reef, the bottom of the boat was in imminent danger of being punctured.

"Now what?" growled Amber. (It should be mentioned that having experienced many previous incidents of this kind with me on a variety of sailboats, running aground was not her favorite thing. In fact, she HATED it.)

I got in the dinghy with a spare anchor and paddled toward deeper water back in the channel. I dropped the spare there and got it set. Back aboard with the new anchor line around a winch, we tried for hours to winch the boat off the reef. It wouldn't budge.

Meanwhile, Amber cleverly managed to untangle the anchor line from the keel and pull it in—an operation that seemed like it took hours. Pulling up the line, we found that in the critical part of the anchor, below the big metal hoop, a huge live conch was trapped. The critter had apparently gotten caught when the tide turned, preventing the anchor from resetting, and setting us adrift.

With both anchors reset, and the conch back in its underwater kingdom, we avoided a long drift to Portugal but still spent a tense and miserable night, with our keel continuing to bang against sharp and hard things underwater. When the tide came in, we popped off the reef like a cork.

There was no savior in this story, except the tide.

It was during another epic grounding, near Cumberland Island, Georgia, that I met my anchoring *deus ex machina*.

I was taking a friend's boat south. Amber was—fortunately—not with me. My friend Sally Taylor was co-captain and shares some of the blame for the ridiculous mess.

We entered a small creek next to Cumberland Island to anchor for the night. Sally and I got into a dispute about where the anchor should go. She said over there, and I said over here. The fussing went on for a while, but as anyone who knows Sally knows, you don't win an argument with that girl. She sued half her family over a property rights dispute and beat them all. Of course, she easily won the argument with me about where to anchor.

Halfway through the night, as the tide was going out—and they have extremely high tides there—I woke up. I had fallen out of my port side bunk. The boat was completely on dry land, resting peacefully on its starboard side.

Safely ensconced in the V berth in the front of the boat and protected from falling out of bed, Sally was laughing uproariously (and rather less than empathetically) at my predicament. She continued giggling and not taking things seriously for the rest of the day.

Here is a photo of the situation.

Boat aground on Cumberland Island

We walked around the dried-out boat for a while, and then I called Towboat US in Hilton Head—and met my *deus ex machina*. He said: "I will be down in about six hours, when the tide floods." So we explored Cumberland Island on foot for about six hours. Our savior came at high tide and dragged us to deeper water. Another black mark for Captain Runaground!

A second grounding occurred in the same vicinity, a year after the first, on *Echo II* as Amber and I were transiting a narrow channel on Thanksgiving Day. (We missed Thanksgiving dinner. But that's another story . . .)

The same Towboat US captain showed up to tow us off. He now knew me by my first name. Before he headed back to his home port on Hilton Head Island, he said, "Good luck, Pope, and I will see you next year."

THE POTATO

In my fifties, I returned to ocean sailing—and to misadventures that, if it weren't for some lucky breaks, could have rivaled, or surpassed, the Fort Pierce shipwreck.

On one occasion, I again found myself on a sailboat filling up with gallons and gallons of water—this time, farther south in the Atlantic Ocean, on the edge of the Caribbean Sea. The thru hull in the forward head had blown out completely, hose and all.

It looked like Old Faithful down in the cabin. With the volume of water that was flooding in through the hull at that rate, the boat was definitely going to sink.

I hurriedly gathered what little safety gear we had. Everyone threw on life vests and harnesses. I found some flares. The life raft was hopelessly buried on deck below the dinghy, so we left it there. Despite my intention to carry the best emergency gear available on any ocean voyage, the boat I was on was severely lacking in that kind of gear.

When the leak blew open, we were nearly a hundred miles from anywhere, on an open-ocean passage from the British Virgin Islands (B.V.I.s) to St. Maarten (the Dutch side of St. Martin)—a two-day trip at most. The area we were transiting was notoriously rough, known as the Anegada Passage. I glanced at the chart. I told the skipper, "There is no island anywhere nearby. St. Croix is the closest, but it is a long way away."

Meanwhile one of the crew, Jim, was desperately stuffing rags in the hole to reduce the water flow. It wasn't working.

"This is not looking good," I thought to myself. "We have got to plug that hole with something solid. And fast!"

I looked around the cabin for something we could use. Anything. We had none of the standard wooden or rubber leak plugs intended for just such an emergency. Suddenly, I saw a sack of potatoes hanging in the galley. I grabbed the biggest potato and tossed it to Jim.

"Here! Try this," I yelled.

Jim caught the potato and immediately stuffed it down in the hole. He pounded it in with every ounce of strength he had.

The flow stopped. "It's holding," he exclaimed. "But I don't know for how long."

We bailed and sailed, reaching the harbor on the Dutch side of St.

Maarten late the next day, February 2, 2011. The same potato was still stuffed in the hole. It had completely stopped the leak.

When I had signed onto this passage, I had answered an ad without asking any questions. The skipper had purchased a 50-foot Beneteau sailboat, and I had signed up as a volunteer member of his delivery crew, to take it from Tortola to St. Maarten. I wanted to get out of the cold weather in Washington, D.C., and go sailing. The owner mentioned that he had sailed on a long ocean voyage with someone else I knew—a skilled, reliable sailor. After hearing that, I had made no further attempt to check his references or qualifications. Bad decision.

It was late in the day on January 31 when I arrived in Tortola, and I was happy to feel the warm breeze. When I exited the taxi from the airport at Hodges Creek in Maya Cove, however, I got my first surprise. I thought, "Oh boy! This is not what I expected. Did I make a mistake to sign up for this?"

Hodges Creek and Maya Cove consisted of a huge bedraggled boat junkyard, a jumble of sinking and broken boats of all kinds and from all over the world, in various stages of decay. Boat parts were scattered around the shoreline. I could smell oil and diesel fuel and the acidic odor of burning plastic.

It wasn't long before I began to suspect that the skipper was not in this game for fun or adventure. He was a quiet, somewhat mysterious man from California who claimed to be a descendant of Genghis Khan. He was definitely not on the up and up. "I am guessing that he is on the run," I thought to myself when I heard him mention a large bank in California where he had been the C.F.O., Chief Financial Officer. That bank was under federal indictment.

The skipper's plan appeared to be staying on the move by boating from one obscure foreign island to another. "He is trying to keep ahead of the FBI," I supposed. The Feds probably wanted to interview him about his involvement in the notorious scandal. He had fled California just before the bank imploded. The bank was found guilty of defrauding the federal mortgage giants, Fannie Mae and Freddie Mac, during the sub-prime mortgage crisis.

The skipper had bought the big Beneteau sailboat from a charter operation in Road Town, in the B.V.I.s. It was only three years old, but he got a special deal because the boat had been used hard in charter operations and had been poorly maintained. We tried to check everything out before we left Tortola to ensure that the boat was seaworthy, but the skipper was in a hurry to move on. With a boat history like that, in a place like Maya Cove, you never know.

I did look the boat over for safety equipment and found it was scarce; well below the minimum. We had almost none of the standard emergency gear. For some reason lost to memory, I boarded anyway.

At first the trip was great fun. We overlooked minor defects in the boat and the scarcity of gear. The other crew members, Jim and Geoff, were hard-living, fun-loving, carefree, and somewhat reckless New Englanders, both of whom lived on sailboats year round. I was in my late sixties. They were 30 years younger than me, and a lot wilder. I could tell immediately that I had a lot to learn from those two about partying—if I could survive it. They were heavy drinkers. They loved pornography and off-color jokes. They knew, or pretended to know, a lot about boat mechanics and women. Sailboat safety and offshore sailing skills were not their thing, however.

I had never before sailed with a team like this. Geoff insisted that he be referred to as the boat's C.P.O., Chief Pussy Officer. I certainly was in no position to dispute that title, given all the amazing tales he told about his escapades back home. He was indeed a good-looking guy in a disreputable sort of way, a "chick magnet" in his words. I was referred to as G.O.M., Grumpy Old Man. Jim started the trip as C.F.H., Chief Fucking Helmsman.

The Chief Fucking Helmsman was at the wheel when we left Maya Cove. He was not fully in charge of his senses when we pulled away from the dock, however. Although it was early in the day, he had already finished at least one bottle of wine and a few hits of rum. In the excitement of departure, Jim neglected to unplug the shore power cable. The boat suddenly lurched and then briefly stopped. The heavy electrical cable connecting the boat to the onshore electrical system snapped with a "boom" as we pulled away. Lots of sparks.

So much for shore power.

Losing the ability to charge the battery from shore power was definitely a problem, because the alternator was showing only 10 volts, not enough to charge a battery.

The skipper was inexperienced in managing sailboats, but he knew a major problem when he saw one. After Jim's embarrassing power cable fiasco, the skipper fired him as C.F.H. and designated me to take the wheel for the rest of our docking and undocking around Tortola before leaving the B.V.I.s. Luckily, I never hit anything or broke anything. But then—I never attempted to drive the boat around crowded harbors while dead drunk.

We sailed over to Spanish Town on the tiny island of Virgin Gorda to get a new power cable and officially check out of the B.V.I.s. with passport and customs authorities. Then we were off to the little island of Anegada north of Tortola.

Anegada is a tiny flat island exposed to the weather from all sides. Periodically, the island gets even flatter as everything above ground gets blown away by storms and hurricanes—houses, trees, utility lines, people—everything. Apart from rubble, there is not much there. Jim, however, discovered one lonely, blown-out, open-air bar in a tent. Jim and Geoff took a lease on the best seats in the tent and spent the entire day attacking the local rum supply.

Next up was a trip around the north of Anegada and then south offshore, avoiding the nasty shoals off the eastern part of the Virgin Islands. I checked the radio weather before we left Anegada. It did not look great to me: 20- to 25-knot east winds and 10-foot waves. When I mentioned the wave forecast to the skipper, he said: "It's probably always like that. A rough passage. That's why I brought you along." Somehow that response did not make me feel all that comfortable.

Geoff put out fishing lines as we rounded the north shore of Anegada and caught a few grouper. Unfortunately, like everything else this crew did, the fishing effort ended badly. Geoff hooked a big tuna. The fish was hard to subdue on the small afterdeck of the Beneteau. As Geoff struggled to keep the large fish onboard, it flipped in a way that drove one prong of the three-prong fish hook right through Geoff's hand. The fish was still alive and kicking, further ripping up his hand. The smell of blood and dying fish was nauseating. It took three of us an hour to get that hook out. Geoff's hand was a bloody mess.

The tuna was good eating, though, even without cooking.

We continued on without Geoff, who went below to get bandages and take some pain killers with a rum additive.

The 10-foot waves were manageable because they were spaced far apart and not steep, but they were enough to make both the C.P.O. and the original C.F.H. seasick. Both were puking overboard soon after we entered the Anegada Passage. But the skipper and I were fine.

When we limped into the harbor on St. Maarten, we motored straight to the yacht yard. The mechanics got a good laugh when they saw the potato. They hauled the boat out immediately and replaced the seacock the same day. They also had a chuckle when they saw our bilge pump. It was pathetic. Barely enough power to pump out a shower.

The mechanic announced: "All the thru hulls are bad, corroded out. This boat is unsafe to sail. It needs to have everything under water replaced. There is rotten metal in everything underwater."

We were lucky that only one thru hull had blown out—although we did have a large sack of potatoes!

The boat owner was looking at some big, unanticipated shipyard bills. I didn't feel too bad for him, though, because I figured the money he was spending probably was not really his.

CHASED BY BULLS IN THE AZORES

> *Mankind faces a crossroads. One path leads to despair and utter hopelessness. The other, to total extinction. Let us pray we have the wisdom to choose correctly.*
> —Woody Allen, "My Speech to the Graduates,"
> *The New York Times*, August 10, 1979

In my case, I have always chosen a third path other than the two envisioned by Woody Allen. My path in life was the one that I hoped would provide the most fun. Often the search for fun has led me to some perilous situations. Not total destruction. Yet.

Take, for example, my sailing trip through the stunningly beautiful Azorean archipelago.

I describe the sailing part of that trip elsewhere, in the story Captains Courageous. The trip was, more or less, the kind of fun anyone could have sailing with a blind captain, a broken foot, unpredictable 15-foot waves, 35-mph winds, volcanic islands with rocky shorelines, and minuscule harbors that you could not imagine squeezing into with a bathtub rubber ducky—let alone a large boat—without crashing into something.

No, the sailing part was only run-of-the mill fun.

The most interesting part was how people in the Azores choose to have fun.

What they do, more or less on a weekly basis, is release a herd of angry bulls out onto the town streets without warning, at least without any warning to English-speaking tourists like me.

How they make the bulls so angry is a state secret, but I am guessing that they poke them in the balls with a long stick or something like that. Anyway, they get exceedingly pissed off at humans. The streets in Azorean towns are narrow, with high walls on either side. Some house fronts are right on the street with little or no sidewalks. I think this is because, up until about 10 years ago, the streets were mostly used by horses and horse carts. It's not all that modern a place.

The upshot of this venue is that any bull in the street gets a really good shot at any idiot human standing in the same street.

Normally, this would have been no problem for me, because until recently I could outrun angry bulls, at least in my imagination.

However, I had broken my foot falling down on a different boat before the trip, and I was wearing a clumsy plastic cast. This left me at a huge disadvantage when all the other fun-loving pedestrians took off, running away from the bulls as fast as they could, and jumping over walls into their front yards.

I stumbled along, not having that much fun, until it was just one bull and me at street level. At first, I thought I could best him by playing possum. I could lie down on the street, I thought, and act like I was a worthless corpse. Another idea was to climb one of the walls. I elected the latter because—who knows if the bull might satisfy his lust for fun by throwing a worthless American corpse around?

So up the wall I scrabbled, not too effectively in my heavy cast. Fortunately, two merciful and hefty Portuguese fishermen got me by the shoulders. My saviors!

Victory! I thumbed my nose at the bull, feeling a massive flood of adrenaline.

Unfortunately, I do not have any close-up pictures of the bull, because by the time he was really close, it was time to pocket the camera and plan an escape.

Here is the secret I discovered that day: you can have fun in any culture, doing things the locals do that you might not do on a daily basis at home—as long as you can get that adrenaline going.

Unlike other bull fights, the Azorean kind are fair, because the bull can also find ways to have fun.

I wish to thank the two Azorean men who lifted me out of range of the bull. Next time I see them, I plan to buy both of them a case of beer.

Also, thanks are due to the skillful—though blind—British captain and crew of the yacht, *Indaba*. They successfully navigated the Lilliputian Azorean harbors without running aground one single time or hitting any other hard objects, while I watched the maneuvers anxiously, with my life vest safely attached, prepared to jump off and swim at the first crunch of fiberglass.

The trip had a lot of potential for disaster. But I managed to choose the correct path—that is, the fun path—every time.

CAPTAINS COURAGEOUS

I have been fortunate to go sailing with interesting people. Before I bought my own cruising sailboat, I sailed across oceans and around various parts of the world with experienced sailors who knew more than I did. I signed up on websites where captains advertised for crew. This produced some enticing offers.

A lot of captains need crew to help deliver boats from one spot to another, mostly along the Atlantic coast and in the Caribbean, since it is unwise to sail in the ocean alone, especially at night and on long trips. This was fertile ground for me. I got a berth on boats going from Annapolis, my home port, to many places, or returning from them: Maine, Cape Cod, the Bahamas, the Virgin Islands and other Caribbean islands, Bermuda, the Panama Canal, and even across the Atlantic to Europe. I did this for a few years and learned a lot, not just about ocean sailing and different sailboats, but also about the kinds of people who like to take long ocean voyages.

The most interesting captain I ever crewed for was an Englishman who advertised for crew for a trip around the Azores. I had sailed to the Azores from Martinique once with another captain, Lee Adamson, but had to leave the islands the same day we arrived due to problems at home.

I desperately wanted to visit the Azores again and explore the beautiful islands I had missed. I was ecstatic to find online a sailor planning to tour all the Azores islands. As I was signing up for the trip, the captain said in an email to me, "Full disclosure. I am totally blind and have been blind since birth. But don't worry, I sailed my boat from England to the Caribbean, and I will be sailing back, with a stopover in the Azores. My crew is leaving the boat there, and that's why I need another crew."

Well, it was pretty clear that he really did need crew, so I signed on. About a week before the departure date, I slipped on an icy dock and broke my foot. I had to wear a big heavy cast and lost most of my mobility. I wrote to the blind Englishman, apologizing and saying that I would have to drop out. He wrote back saying, "No way. Come anyway. I have no other crew and we will make a great pair of disabled sailors."

So I went. And we did.

The Azores were fabulous, one of my best sailing trips anywhere, and the blind captain was amazingly resourceful and skillful. We encountered some pretty rotten weather, but he was tuned in to all the European weather forecasts, so at least we knew what we were getting into.

The biggest problem for me was steering the boat into strange little fishing-boat harbors on the islands that were not visited by yachts. Obviously the blind captain was not involved in the steering. Local knowledge would have been very helpful, but I don't speak Portuguese. And I doubt anyone was monitoring any VHF radio channels, assuming we even knew which channel to tune to, which we did not.

We survived all of the tricky entrances, visited every single Azorean island, and took car tours of all of them. Millions of hydrangeas were in bloom. From time to time I hear from the captain, who is still sailing around England. An amazing guy, and I felt fortunate to have the opportunity to sail with him. (For more about this trip, see the story about the bulls.)

It was going to be hard to top that Azorean trip, but then I got a crew gig on a boat leaving Aruba and heading for Panama via the Venezuelan and Colombian coast—a zone infested with drugs and pirates. The appeal for me was the San Blas Islands off the Panama Coast. I badly wanted to visit them.

But what about this captain? Again, as we were negotiating my crew job, there was another unsettling disclosure. He wrote, "I am pretty agile, but I lost one of my legs in a mountain-climbing accident. I still have the other one, and I have a prosthetic leg." He wasn't kidding. He had part of his missing leg but not much. Unfortunately, the prosthetic device was made out of a metal that kept getting rusty in the ocean air. He survived on WD-40.

Again, this was another captain made of steel. Or possibly aluminum. We left Aruba and aimed for Cartagena, Colombia. The problem, as experienced sailors know, was that the Venezuelan coast is infested with pirates, and the Colombian coast has the worst weather in the Caribbean.

Luckily, we did not get hit by the pirates (thanks to the gods), but we did get hit by the weather. A sudden powerful storm came up, and we needed to immediately reduce sail. Unfortunately, the boat had in-mast roller furling for the mainsail, which works well when the wind is not blowing, but not so well when the wind is blowing hard. A vertical batten got jammed in the mast slot as we were trying to wind it in with the electric machine inside the mast. The machine got fried. This left us with a sail tearing apart in a huge wind, only partially furled, and the boat not liking the situation at all. Finally we got the sail to partially collapse by hauling up on the topping lift. But the mainsail was wrecked and so was the furling machinery.

We went to the San Blas Islands anyway, and I had a wonderful time while the captain agonized about how to get repairs. Finally, I had to leave the boat and the island paradise to fly home. Getting from the San Blas Islands to an airport in Panama was another amazing experience, involving a dug-out log canoe and a lot of jungle travel.

The San Blas trip was not the last one with a partially disabled captain. Another sailor wanted to take his brand new Dufour sailboat from the Chesapeake Bay to the Virgin Islands. After I signed on, he disclosed that he had neurological problems from catching Lyme disease and not having it treated fast enough. He had partial paralysis on his left side and could not legally drive a car. Also, he tended to pass out suddenly. By this time, I was getting used to captains' physical problems.

The trip would have been great, and the captain's problems were not bad at all, except for the fact that we lost the full use of our rudder in the middle of the trip, halfway from the Chesapeake to the Virgin Islands. Our steering problems got so severe that we never got to the Virgins. We ended up in Puerto Rico, and I flew home. He eventually got the rudder fixed, and I went on some other trips with him later. A great guy to sail with.

The only bad trip I had with an exotic captain was a charter trip I took with my partner, Amber, and my travel buddy, Jack Hession. We were going to tour the Windward Islands in the Caribbean with a paid captain, instead of someone I would have to assist. It was going to be luxurious and relaxing, and Amber was all for that. He was a Dutch guy, an experienced sailor. We signed up and paid our deposits.

Then we got an email from the captain, informing us that on his way from the Netherlands to Martinique, where he was scheduled to meet us, he had had an accident in the Canary Islands. He had crashed his boat into a jetty outside a harbor, damaging the hull. He and his wife had to be evacuated by helicopter. He wrote, "I hope you have travel insurance because I have no money to return your deposit."

We had no travel insurance. But what could we do?

Several weeks later, we got another email saying that he had gotten the boat fixed and was crossing the Atlantic to the Caribbean soon. He wanted to resume the trip if we were still available. We were, and we flew down to Martinique.

When we started sailing around the islands with this guy, I realized why he had crashed into the harbor jetty in the Canaries. He got up in the morning and started on a bottle of rum and never stopped all day. Also, he sailed the boat as if he was in a race for his life.

So much for the drunken Dutch captain.

Amber offered an additional comment about this cruise: "This captain cleverly arranged, in advance, for the paying passengers to cover the cost of the captain's share of the food and drink, including alcohol. It wasn't just rum he imbibed; on some days, the captain, with the help of a Dutch passenger, tore through two cases of beer before 5 pm. At the passengers' expense."

SAILBOAT RACING ON THE CHESAPEAKE (ARE WE HAVING FUN YET?)

The best cure for seasickness is to sit under a tree.
—traditional saying

This is the story (one elderly sailor's story, anyway) of the Annapolis-to-Baltimore Race and the follow-up race the next day (the Francis Scott Key Race) on the weekend of October 19-20, 2019. I was on *Atlas*, a 40-foot C&C skippered by Peter (the Punster) Holden, with a crew of Shelley Castle, Ann Ruppel, and me.

The question that kept coming to mind all weekend, although no one voiced it, was: "Are we having fun yet?" A more existential version is: "Why are we doing this?"

Basically, this was one very screwed-up series of two races. The races were screwed up mostly by weather, but the Race Committee also played a part. It was a bit of a mess from beginning to end, punctuated only by an unusually good after-race party on Saturday night.

We started out Saturday morning, just a bit north of the Chesapeake Bay Bridge near Maryland Light, headed north. Expectations were high. But the forecast was for winds of 2 knots, with an adverse current. A sailboat cannot easily sail against a current in wind that light.

Sadly, the forecast was spot on.

Before the start, the Race Committee boat roamed the Bay to find a good starting point for the race. They motored around the Bay, up the Bay, and down the Bay, with more than 40 sailboats motoring behind like little ducklings.

Finally the geniuses on the Race Committee settled on a spot, put the anchor down, and posted the race courses for various fleets on some miniature postage stamps attached to the side of the boat, for all of the crews to read—with binoculars, I guess. The spot they chose to start the race was about the worst imaginable for the course they set, but . . . never mind, the race got started.

Each fleet had a start time five minutes after the start of the previous fleet. "Boom" went the start cannon for the first fleet. There was massive confusion on everyone's part as to which fleet was racing which course.

The first fleet charged the starting line at 0.03 knots against the current. Five minutes later our fleet started, charging the line at the same awesome speed. But, of course, the entire first fleet was still there, stymied by the lack of wind and adverse current. It was a short start line, getting extremely crowded with the boats from two fleets attempting to move forward with little success. Then, five minutes later, came the third fleet; and five minutes later, the fourth. Most of the first fleet, and second fleet, etc., were still struggling to get across the start line.

You get the idea. A clusterfuck. Lots of yelling. Lots of engines turned on to avoid collisions, lots of protests. We were constantly pushing other boats away by hand.

Finally, enough wind showed up to move boats up the course beyond the start line. The wind continued to build as the day went on, making it possible for each fleet to finish its race course. Our boat, *Atlas,* was doing well in the bigger breeze, and was probably even in first place, until a nasty time-consuming boo-boo moved us back to third place on the podium.

The boo-boo was caused by the jib trimmers imperfectly coordinating the release and haul-in of the jib sheets during a jibe. One sheet trimmer fully released the starboard sheet before the other trimmer wound the port sheet in, causing the whole jib to blow forward and wrap itself tightly around the forestay.

Unwinding this took a few minutes, costing *Atlas* the supreme victory.

Then there was the party. As always, sailing tales were invented and reinvented, and plenty of food and drink was eaten and drunk.

I looked so forlorn at the entrance (see photo) that one of the event staff slipped me a free food ticket. I immediately went off on an eating binge, gorging on chicken to the point where I could feel feathers growing. I thought, I might lay an egg if I ate another drumstick.

The author on the dock in Baltimore

The rest of the ambitious *Atlas* squad went ashore on an extensive restaurant search while I belched and farted, trying to digest an entire chicken.

Eating a big meal was fortuitous, because the next day, food would be scarce. It was raining like hell as we got ready for the second race. The rain didn't stop all day. As crew member Blake Slavin later put it, it was "soaking, wringing, dripping, drenching, saturated wet . . . bone-chilling, prune-toed, hair-plastering wet."

The wind was blowing 15 knots per hour and gusting higher. Visibility sucked.

This is where good rain gear comes in handy. My old secondhand gear (donated by my old friend and veteran sailor Sally Taylor) leaked in every possible spot. I was wet to the bone almost immediately and shivering.

Only six boats showed up in our group. Apparently, the word was out around the docks: "Don't race in this mess." We never got the word.

Down the Bay we sailed in the fog, on a beam reach, heeled over with the boom almost in the water. Ann had jumped ship, replaced by Blake Slavin and John, the Canadian. I moved my massive frame, weighing in at 145 pounds, to the windward side of the boat, trying to balance the boat—to no avail.

This soaking misery went on for several hours until we finally made it to the finish line. At that point, the boat was wet but otherwise in good shape.

The damages came soon thereafter. We headed home to Lake Ogleton, dead downwind under the Bay Bridge. Then, just after the bridge, we suffered an accidental jibe, the jib and main sails violently sweeping across the boat. This tore out some of the critical equipment on the boat—the traveler and the preventer. But everyone was still on board and still had heads on their necks. Life jackets were quietly donned at that point.

Next we tried to reel in the jib. That required luffing it to take off the pressure (which was substantial now). So luff it we did. The subsequent flogging in the strong breeze tore up the sail, delaminating parts of it and ripping it in several places.

Then we moved to the main sail. So far, it was still more or less in one piece, but it needed to come down too. Another luffing episode ensued, and the main had its chance to try to flog itself to pieces. I think it suffered only one tear.

The damage was beginning to mount, but now we were on the way home under power. Still soaking wet.

My worst moment occurred when I suddenly felt something wet going down my legs. I thought, "I must be pissing in my pants! How humiliating!"

The liquid kept coming until it filled up both of my boots and started overflowing. Then I thought, "Wait a minute. This is a hell of a lot of very cold liquid. It can't be pee." A little investigating proved there was a huge leak in the rear of my rain gear, funneling gallons of rainfall down the inside of my pants, down my legs, and into my boots.

Time for some new rain gear. And pray for some sun for my next sailboat race.

CLOSE CALL ON THE DREADED C&D CANAL

I seemed to have a propensity for finding questionable boats and captains.

On one occasion, the captain of the sailboat I was a passenger on ran into a railroad bridge.

We hit the bridge so hard that I almost fell off the stern. The captain, Dave, gripped the wheel tightly as the boat tilted, bow up in the air, and the mast became entangled in the bridge structure. Another crew member struggled to get up the stairs of the companionway to the cockpit, but with the boat pointed at the sky, the rush of water flushing in from the stern kept washing him backwards.

"This does not look good," I thought to myself.

My sailing friend Dave liked to take his boat every year from the Chesapeake Bay up to Martha's Vineyard, where he had a summer home. He invited me to go along for one of those trips. For many sailors the preferred route would be an offshore, ocean trip, direct from the Chesapeake Bay to Block Island and then to the Vineyard. An alternative route is an ocean trip up the New Jersey coast to Long Island Sound and then east to the Vineyard. I had done both of those routes several times before.

Sailing offshore normally requires sleeping and eating aboard for multiple days and nights. The problem on this trip was that Dave did not like to cook and eat aboard. This meant that either we starved—and Dave was not up for that—or we found a place to dine ashore EVERY SINGLE NIGHT.

In order to do that, Dave took a totally different route.

Dave found places to stop for dinner along the way that I never imagined were possible. Barnegat, New Jersey, for one; and then Shinnecock on the south side of Long Island. Entering those harbors can be dangerous for large sailboats. I was nervous as hell about sailing into either of them for the night, in any kind of weather, but Dave was not going to miss his daily dinners on shore. We did make it in and out of both of them, and had fabulous meals at both. But I don't think I ever want to take that route again.

Our first stop after leaving the Chesapeake Bay was, naturally, a dinner stop. It was in the Chesapeake and Delaware (C&D) canal. We had a great dinner at the marina in the canal and stayed overnight. We needed to leave early the next day to catch the strong current in the canal at a good tide level.

We started out immediately upon waking up. Our starting score was inauspicious. Coffee: 0. Breakfast: 0. Situational awareness: near 0. One crew member was still dozing in his bunk.

We turned the corner from the marina into the canal and headed east, being swept rapidly along by a powerful eastbound current. Shortly beyond the marina entrance is a huge steel railroad bridge that goes up to lets ships through and then down when a train arrives. The bridge had no lights or warning sounds to indicate when it was headed up or down. It was operated remotely from some other place, possibly in the Midwest. Dave assured me that the bridge was usually up. I said, "OK." And I went back to sleepily coiling up the dock lines. Suddenly: "CRASH!"

As we hit the bridge, the strong current pushed us against it. The mast got tangled in the bottom of the bridge. The boat tilted backward, bow up and stern down, then twisted and slid sideways, under the bridge. Fortunately, the bridge was on its way up, not down, and as it continued upward, our boat freed itself from entanglement and slid completely under the bridge. Amazingly, the mast was still standing, though badly damaged.

That was dumb luck.

The rest of the trip was uneventful, despite an unusable mast that forced us to motor—and despite all those dinners ashore each night.

That was not my last terrifying experience in the C&D Canal, however. The current in the canal is so strong that, in a sailboat, you need to plan your trip to move only with, not against, the current. This sometimes requires waiting as long as six hours for the current to shift. The same is not true for large, powerful commercial vessels, which can lead to some dangerous confrontations.

On a trip with my friend Mike Tabor, a captain I have sailed with many times in many places, we were headed west in the canal, moving with the current. It was one of the darkest nights imaginable. Mike was exhausted, having been awake all day and the previous night during a windy offshore trip down the New Jersey coast and then up Delaware Bay.

Mike went below for some shut-eye, and I took the helm. We had no other crew. I was feeling wide awake, but visibility was zero, and the canal has a few bends in it. There is a phone number you can call to check for commercial traffic, but that only operates in daytime—or so we thought at the time.

Proceeding happily down the middle of the canal in the dark, I suddenly saw a light high in the sky, around a bend. I was baffled. What could that be? Then suddenly I realized: it was a huge ship, coming around the bend! I was in the middle of the canal, headed for an imminent collision. Yikes! The ship's crew clearly could not see me and could not maneuver quickly anyway. They were moving fast.

The correct protocol for boats passing in opposite directions is to pass port to port; in other words, staying right and passing left side to left side—like cars. The problem was that, although I was on the correct side of the canal, he was on the same side! With no time to fuss about rules and rights of way, I had no choice but to turn left and aim for the opposite, left bank of the canal—crossing directly in front of the speeding ship—in order to pass him on our starboard, or right, side.

Holding my breath, I pushed the accelerator to the max and jerked the wheel all the way over. I drove directly for the left bank, preferring to crash into the bank than to be hit by tons of fast-moving steel. We barely made it across the canal in front of the ship before it reached us, passing within a few feet. I was sweating profusely, but the boat crew probably never knew we were there.

That was the last trip I ever took at night through that canal or any other one. After that, whenever I approached the C&D Canal, I initiated frequent, and extensive, conversations with the ship traffic controller in Chesapeake City before entering the canal. I refused to enter the canal at night if there was any commercial traffic AT ALL.

Luck can only carry you so far.

9
IT WAS NOT ALL FUN

COUSIN ARTHUR

Not everything we did on the farm as kids was fun. I killed my cousin when I was 9 years old.

I did not mean to kill him. I did not want to kill him. It was an accident.

At age 9 I was living on our small, debt-ridden dairy farm in Maryland, where I grew up. We kids were part of the labor force on the farm whenever we were not in school. On one occasion I was entrusted, unwisely as it turns out, with the task of bringing a load of hay bales into the barn from the hayfield up on a hill across the road, some distance from the barn. This meant that I got to drive the tractor. I could hardly reach the controls, but I was very puffed up about this adult responsibility.

It was a hot, dusty, sweaty September day. Labor was scare on our farm, and one of my mother's elderly relatives, "Cousin Arthur" as he was known to us, was helping out despite his advanced age. He was a small man, old and rather fragile. Nevertheless, he enjoyed participating as best he could in farm work, especially sitting up high on top of the bales of fresh sweet-smelling hay in the blazing sun as we brought the hay wagon in from the field.

While driving the tractor to haul the wagon in from the hay field,

I went down a steep hill, going too fast. The wagon hit a bump. Cousin Arthur tumbled off the top of the hay and hit the ground hard. I heard a loud thump.

He had landed on his head. Never regained consciousness.

My parents tried to convince me that it wasn't my fault. But I knew in my heart that I had killed a sweet old man whom I was extremely fond of.

This is not a good memory to have lurking in your subconscious for 70 years. It was also the beginning of a lifetime of bad decisions.

FEAR AND LOATHING AT LISBON ELEMENTARY

I became a nerd early. In elementary school. It was fear that did it.

My mother was always going on about how important it was to do well in school and get good grades. Her chief tactic was to try to scare the crap out of me and my brothers about the consequences that would ensue if we did not get good grades. I made the huge mistake of being taken in by this scare tactic. I was terrified. My brothers never fell for the scare tactics. My gullibility led to 20 years of living a life someone else had envisioned for me and never knowing what the heck it was all about.

We were all enrolled in the Lisbon Elementary School in Lisbon, Maryland, when the scare tactics began in earnest. Lisbon Elementary was not a top-of-the-line school. Almost all the students there were farm kids who worked on the farms in the morning before school. We had no time to clean up before school, so the classrooms smelled like cow shit and rotting silage.

Lisbon Elementary School sign

Across the street from the school there was a run-down, rickety little gas station. When we went to school across the street in the 1940s and 1950s, working at the gas station was a low-level job. In those days you were not allowed to pump your own gas. Usually some poor guy who had no discernible skills would do it for you. These guys never looked wealthy. My mother would always point to the gas station when we drove by and say: "If you don't get good grades, you are going to end up pumping gas over there!"

Neither of my younger brothers was fooled, even a little bit, by this scare tactic. But I was. Driven by existential fear, I went crazy through elementary and high school trying to be first in my class, or at least close to it. I was terrified of having to pump gas for the rest of my life. I became a major nerd and studied my ass off.

My brother Henry recently reminded me that he sometimes asked me to come out and play with him during the days when we were in Lisbon Elementary. I replied, "I can't. I am busy memorizing the dictionary." I really got into that task and became virtually a "walking dictionary." I also read through the entire Encyclopedia Britannica.

Early on in school, I began to realize that the whole school thing was a kind of a game. Students and teachers each had distinct roles. If you learned all the techniques and rules, you could get very good at playing the game—and avoid a lifetime of pumping gas. The game needed to be played hard and taken seriously. It was a lot like playing poker well. You had to learn a lot of stuff which you had no interest in and which, in essence, was totally meaningless and useless other than helping you win. It did not lead to insight, wisdom, or anything profound like that.

If I were a reflective person, I would suggest that perhaps our educational system needs re-imagining. Perhaps we could have a system in which individual talents were recognized and enhanced. But . . . don't get me started.

Most kids did not want to bother with learning the tricks of classroom learning. Some didn't even recognize it as a game. They just wanted to get it over with and go outside to play. But not me. Fear of ending up at the gas station drove me deep into mastering the game.

In college and graduate school, the game was not much different. People think you are smart, even if you aren't, if you master some of the tricks and techniques that make things go your way. Once you learn to write reasonably well, for example, you can pass almost any essay exam even if you have not studied the materials or gone to class. Other tricks and techniques include learning how to speed read a book and still manage to remember everything in it; how to write an essay about something you have no knowledge of; how to hack multiple-choice tests.

Most intellectually average and below-average people, like me, struggle academically in high school, college, and graduate school because they have not learned the games, the tricks, and the techniques. They don't learn how memory works, so they immediately forget what they think they have studied. They don't master the trick of how to take notes for total recall and maximum comprehension. And worst of all, they don't know how to kiss the teacher's ass.

Some other people may be brilliant and have over-the-top IQs, but in taking tests, they may be lost. Such people are like talented athletes trying to play tennis or another sport without knowing the rules or having any technique, tactics, or strategy. Natural ability may result in a few good shots, but in the end, any mediocre player who has learned the tricks and practiced them is going to eat them for lunch.

Again, may I suggest briefly that our entire system of education may need a bit of rethinking. . . .

But on with the story . . .

My mother's fear tactic worked on me from the get-go. I knew I was far, very far, from being smart and so I badly needed to learn how the education game was played. I studied every aspect. I learned how to speed read with much greater comprehension of the material. I mastered ways to remember everything in a textbook. I learned how to get good at test-taking techniques in high school.

I mastered enough of the tricks to get into Yale. There, again, the frightening nightmares returned about the possibility of ending up as a stumble-bum pumping gas. But college turned out to be just a bigger version of high school. In college, in fact, I discovered that some professors would let you in on their game, and even give you blatant hints about the next exam. But you had to meet with the professor in person and plead and beg convincingly, adding, of course, a detailed explanation of how much you loved his class.

After college, the Vietnam War was looming. I did not want to go to Vietnam and end up in a body bag. So I applied to Harvard Law School for the sole purpose of keeping my student draft deferment. I got accepted. There, the rules for getting ahead were different. It took me a year to figure them out.

Somewhere along the line in law school, however, the fear of pumping gas began to wear off. I stopped caring about beating the system. I had the degrees and transcripts, but I felt like I had not learned anything of value. I had little or no common sense. I was immature and totally irresponsible. In personal relationships, I was hopelessly lost. I had long ago lost sight of what was right and wrong.

There are such things as emotional intelligence and wisdom. I had so little of those that I could not even have described what they were.

On the big pie of intelligence, I was the master of only a tiny slice, the slice that involved taking tests and writing essays. The rest of the pie was terra incognita to me. None of what I was doing was making me a better person. Nor was I on a path to happiness.

I thought to myself, "I need to somehow get free from this nightmare. It was a huge mistake which has left me on a treadmill to nowhere."

Then I found out about LSD. It was widely available in Cambridge, the home of Richard Alpert and Timothy Leary, both professors at Harvard at that time. A few doses of that stuff clarified the whole picture for me.

The fog lifted. I saw clearly the academic game for what it was. I could still play it, but . . . why bother?

Only a year or two after law school, I totally dropped off the treadmill, left my job in the "normal" world, and started a search across the world for the sources of wisdom and the ultimate meaning of life. Those adventures are recounted elsewhere in this book.

Many years later, I was at the Lisbon gas station to get my car fixed. A young guy in his twenties took my order. We chatted briefly. He seemed intelligent and competent. And apparently happy. I pointed across the street to Lisbon School and told him, "I went to elementary school right over there." He said, "So did I."

We both had a little chuckle and said no more.

BEHIND BARS

Sometimes, someone unexpected comes into your life out of nowhere and makes your heart beat faster and changes you forever. We call those people "cops."
—unknown

I woke up to the sound and smell of vomit. I was in the drunk tank in a filthy, stinking jail. I had a brutal hangover, and I was not alone. The other drunks were taking turns throwing up in the toilet. Or near the toilet. I was the best dressed of the lot; I still had on my tuxedo. But I certainly didn't feel much better than the others.

I was only locked up twice in my brief and undistinguished criminal career. The second time doesn't really count because I went into the cell voluntarily for lack of anywhere else to sleep, and I was happy to be there. (That story is told elsewhere in this book.) Not so this first time.

I was in the jail in Westminster, the county seat for Carroll County, Maryland. This county was named after an early founder of the state, Charles Carroll. Because of my mother's vast network of social connections in Maryland, we were loosely associated with the Carroll family. One degenerate offspring of this illustrious family, Harper Carroll, was in love with my mother and would not leave her alone, even after she got married to someone else and had three children. He was a serious drunkard. He would often show up at our farm, completely plastered, and try to get my mother to go off with him somewhere, even as she was trying to get on with her life. She would, of course, down a few pops with him just to be sociable before she ushered him off to his car.

So much for the elite aristocracy of Maryland.

The Carroll connection did not help me much on this particular occasion, but my mother had other connections that were very useful. In fact, it was my mother's social connections that got me into that fix in the first place.

I was 18 years of age, driving west on Liberty Road somewhere near Eldersburg, Maryland, about seven miles from home. I had been to a fancy party at the Elkridge Club in Baltimore and was trying to navigate my way back to the family farm near Sykesville, at least an hour drive from the club. It was late at night and I was feeling the effects of about eight or nine gin and tonics.

How did I get so drunk at only 18? To understand how that happened, and how it happened almost every weekend that year, one must understand one of the peculiar and archaic customs of Baltimore families who considered themselves to be "upper crust" at that time. The custom was called "coming out." It now has a different meaning, but back then it had nothing at all to do with homosexuality. Far from it.

When an upper-crust family's daughter got to a certain age, usually 17 or 18, it was time to introduce her to what her parents considered "polite society." She was referred to as a "debutante," and she needed to meet the right kind of boys at the right kind of extravagant event called a "coming-out party," or "debutante party." These were usually held at a prestigious country club, or sometimes at the family's estate in the Greenspring Valley, or some other upscale venue.

Of course, 18-year-old girls in Baltimore in the early 1960s already knew a lot of boys, but most of them were probably not fully "the right kind" of boys—at least not in all the ways that the girls' parents would have hoped. They may have been produced by wealthy families. They may have had awesome cars. They may have been absurdly wealthy. They may have been attending the right private schools. Their families may have been in Maryland since before the American Revolution. But some of these young men were downright sexual predators who would get the drunken debutantes into bushes at the drop of a hat. The parents of these girls seemed totally oblivious to what was going on in the bushes. So the parties went on, with underage girls and boys from the upper crust getting drunk as skunks and behaving like they were at a Roman orgy.

I got involved in this mess through no doing of my own, but once I realized the possibilities, I was all in. Free drinks all night. Music. Drunken young girls looking for a good time. What's not to like?

I did not realize at the time that I was supposed to be upper crust. My life was about as far from the typical wealthy upper class life as it could be. My family was in financially desperate straits throughout my whole childhood. My days involved shoveling cow manure, shooting groundhogs, and beating the crap out of my younger brothers. I was not going to the symphony, ballet, or other cultural events. But my mother was a force of nature. She compensated for our impecunious situation by befriending people in the right places. She was damn well determined that the Barrow boys were going to hang out with the right kind of people from the right families, just as she had done when she was growing up.

My mother, always addressed by others as "Miss Kitty," knew all the social big shots in Baltimore because she had attended a posh girls' high school, Bryn Mawr. This was one of the two or three all-girls schools for upper-crust Baltimoreans. So it was no big problem for her to get our names in a critical address book, called the "Blue Book."

The Blue Book was a semi-secret book containing the names and contact information of all the people in and around Baltimore who were entitled to be considered part of the official upper crust. What the criteria were for getting your information in that book, and who made those decisions, remains, to this day, a mystery to me. We were not Jewish or Italian so I suppose that was the main qualification. In any case, Miss Kitty knew the score, and my brothers and I were in that Blue Book from the day of our birth until mother finally gave up on the whole scheme when we reached the ages of 19 or 20. Around that time she realized, with intense disappointment, that none of us were ever going to follow the Blue Book path.

Going to the debutante parties was a blast for me. My life with the cows and groundhogs on the farm and in miserable summer jobs on the state roads was otherwise pretty boring. To get into the parties, you had to wear a tuxedo with a white dinner jacket, but that was no big deal for our mother, who had a wealthy woman friend with a son older than me. I got his designer hand-me-downs. The major problem for me was getting home to our remote farm after the events. It was more than an hour of drunk driving down unlighted, twisty, two-lane country roads. I would never get home before 2 or 3 am.

The getting-home part was really dangerous for me and for my two brothers, who did this same debutante thing in the years after I aged out of it. My youngest brother, Jake, was the worst of all. To start with, he was a terrible driver even when stone-cold sober. After 20 stiff drinks . . . well . . . you can imagine.

Jake never ended up in jail. However, on one occasion, I was awakened in bed at 3 am by his frantic clawing at me and whispering, "Pope, you gotta help! I had a problem with the car, and I can't get it home. Mother's going to kill me."

So I got up and followed him on foot about two miles down the road. We found the car, a Volkswagen bug, upside down in a cornfield with the roof crushed in. He had taken the turn at a high rate of speed and flipped the car on its top.

We pushed the car back over and, amazingly, drove it home. I said, "What about the top?" Jake replied: "No problem. I am going to push it back out. She will never notice."

He got in the front seat and proceeded to stomp his feet upwards into the car roof until some of it popped back out. In the light of day, it looked like it had been run over by a truck, but in his shape at that time of night, he convinced himself that all was well.

Jake denies some elements of this story but his memories are suspect, since he was drunk at the time. He does admit that he has flipped VW bugs—not once, but three times. His claim is that that there was a design defect in the bug that resulted in flips when one took sharp turns at high speeds. This claim could be fact checked, but

I would need to point out that, regardless of design issues, no one else we knew ever flipped a bug. Not even once.

Jake also succeeded in embarrassing our mother now and then at the debutante parties. On one occasion, my mother got a call one Sunday morning after a debutante party that Jake had attended with my other brother Henry. This was Jake's first debutante party. He was only 15, way under age. He was even too young to drive, so Henry was supposed to be his chaperone.

The morning after the party, the hostess called my mother on the phone and asked, "Kitty, have you noticed anything missing?" Innocently, my mother said, "No. Like what?" The other lady said, "Is your younger son around?"

Mother took a look. No Jake.

Back on the phone, she asked what had happened.

The hostess said, "Well. We were cleaning up after the party for my daughter last night, and we found a person who claims he is one of your boys. He was sleeping in one of the tents under one of the tables. He may be sick. He is covered in vomit. Should we send him home?"

Henry had gone home without Jake. He claims he could not find Jake after searching the entire place. The tables had long white tablecloths that reached all the way down to the ground. Jake was passed out under one of those, covered in puke.

As it turned out, Jake had not even been invited. He had convinced his older brother Henry to let him tag along. Jake was blackballed from future debutante parties after that disturbing incident, but he soon found that getting an invitation was not the key to attending. The key was dressing in the right outfit, being polite to the hosts when you entered, and heading straight to the bar. The hosts were usually too slopped to know, or even care, who you were. Jake claims to have attended dozens of deb parties after being blackballed.

It was on one of my own trips home from this kind of event that I ended up in the hoosegow. I got pulled over by a county cop who observed that my vehicle was going about 20 miles per hour and weaving all over the road. Not only that, but my car had North

Carolina tags. This looked suspicious to the young officer. It was my dad's car and he had registered it in Asheville, North Carolina, where he moved while I was still in high school.

The cop never said a word about the cloud of alcohol fumes emanating from the car window. However, he did ask lots of questions about the car. Apparently, my responses were sufficiently suspicious that he concluded that I was driving a stolen car. So into the county jail I went with a stolen vehicle charge. He didn't bother with any driving-while-drunk issues because, to him, the stolen car was much more of a big deal.

That's where he screwed up. And I got lucky.

I spent the weekend in the tank in Westminster, Maryland, with three local drunks. Got to know the other drunks who were puking all over. It was a mess. My tuxedo never smelled quite right afterwards.

My case came up Monday morning. By that time, my mother had contacted the judge, whom she knew socially because her father, my grandfather, was a judge in the next county over. All the judges knew each other in those days. The trial was a farce. I showed up in my tux with dried puke, but as soon as the judge discovered that the car was not stolen, he started scolding the poor cop and apologizing to me. No one said a thing about my driving while dead drunk.

I went home without even a ticket. My mother had saved my reputation as the "right kind" of boy.

A BETRAYAL OF TRUST

> *Regret . . . it's the second most common emotion.*
> —Amy Summerville, "Regrets, I Have a Few,"
> *Hidden Brain* (podcast), September 11, 2017

I was in tenth grade at a private school in Baltimore when my father found a job in North Carolina and decided to move the whole family down to Asheville. I did not want to go. I wanted to finish high school in the same place I started.

My mother got together with the school and made it all work out for me. I was to live with an elderly couple, Dr. and Mrs. Everett, who lived on Club Road near the school. Their kids had all graduated and gone on to live somewhere else. They were empty nesters, well known to the school, and the mother, especially, was feeling empty. She loved having kids around, even adolescents, and was eager to take me on, since the school vouched for me as a student with good grades and an impeccably good behavior record, so far. I was just getting started, however, and that record was soon to change.

I liked my temporary parents. We had animated discussions about politics and current affairs. I was already a liberal Democrat and they were both rock-ribbed Republicans and evangelicals. But we got along anyway. At least until Sunday.

On my first Sunday morning in their home, Mrs. Everett notified me that I must attend church as a condition of living with them. This was not a welcome announcement. I hated church. I was actually a budding atheist, albeit still in the closet. I have never been able to believe the absurd childish stories of Christianity. Nor could I imagine an unseen unknowable being who created and continues to control everything. However, this view was clearly not going to be acceptable to the Everetts, who had a deep North Carolina Bible Belt evangelical belief system. I wisely avoided the treacherous rocks of the religious coast in conversation. It could only lead to problems.

I could avoid talking about religion, but I had to go to church. I did not want to go. How could I solve this problem? I came up with a story and, of course, a lie. I said that I was deep into the Episcopalian religion of my parents and wanted to go only to their church. The Everetts agreed to that compromise. Thank God for the many denominations available in the Protestant panoply!

So every Sunday, off I trundled to the Episcopal Church nearby while the Everetts went to their Baptist Church. Of course, I never set foot in the church; I just stayed in the parking lot in my dilapidated old jalopy, listening to rock and roll on the radio.

This system worked beautifully for a few weeks. But then I think

Mrs. Everett became suspicious. She asked me what the sermon was about. It was time to think fast. I improvised some story about Jesus performing a miracle and turning water into wine or some such thing. This was obviously not going to work long term. On the other hand, I was determined not to be forced into church.

My backup plan was to go to the church, pick up the little paper at the front door announcing the various scriptures to be read and the title of the sermon. I thought, "I can wing it from that." Maxing out my imagination, I made this work. I don't know if the Everetts believed me, but I know they immensely enjoyed my fanciful and lengthy renditions of the sermons. It worked, and, even better, I learned how to tell a good yarn, a talent which has stood me in good stead ever since.

I got a babysitting job just around the corner from the Everetts' house. It was good money and the Everetts vouched for me. Unfortunately I did not live up to their billing. One evening, the kids were asleep, the parents were still out, and I needed gas in my car. So I reasoned, "I can just go down the street, get some gas, and be back before the parents get home. What could go wrong?" This was a big blunder. I got the gas, but when I got back the parents were home, burning mad. That was my last babysitting job anywhere, ever. Even I realized that I could not be trusted in that situation.

When you have betrayed someone's trust, there is no way out. You have to live with it forever. In this case, I have been angry with myself for more than 60 years.

I was not finished betraying people's trust in me yet. One day in my senior year, the Everetts announced they would be away for the weekend and wanted me to look after the house. I thought to myself, "PARTY TIME!"

The Everetts left town. I invited everyone I knew over to a big house party. Almost the whole senior class came. It was a drunken fiasco. Tons of beer and whiskey. I passed out. It was a mess.

After I passed out, my friends decided to help me out by cleaning up. They packed up all the bottles and cans and other trash and put everything in some cardboard boxes, which they proceeded to throw on a lawn down the street.

The Everetts came home and were none the wiser for a while. I thought I had gotten away with the whole thing. Wrong. The neighbors on whose lawn the trash ended up came by a day or so later. The Everetts' name and address were on one of the boxes. They inquired, "What's up?" I was screwed. I had to confess. I had betrayed their trust.

The Everetts were amazingly forgiving. They let me off the hook, but they let the school know. I was in deep doo-doo there. The headmaster and other teachers convened a disciplinary session, and it looked like I was going to get the boot—in my last year of high school. The class officers of the senior class were convened to ratify my expulsion. This is where my lucky streak hit the jackpot. My high-school friend Henry Hopkins, who had never had a single demerit throughout all of his high-school years and who had taken on the thankless burden of saving my ass from all kinds of idiotic blunders, made a special appeal to the Assistant Headmaster. My mother also pleaded my case with the school authorities.

The clincher was that every single class officer had been at my party, and one or two of them—as well as my friend Henry Hopkins—confessed to having attended the event. This meant that all the officers of the senior class, as well as dozens of others, would also have to be disciplined if I was kicked out. That was a bridge too far for the school. They let me off with a slap on the wrist and admonitions about not doing anything like that again.

I had gotten lucky again. But did I ever live it down? No, not in my own mind. It occupies a sad space in my memory as a total loss of integrity—a betrayal of the Everetts' trust. A stain that is hard to erase.

I grew to love the Everetts. They were as close to me as my own family. I did not realize until Dr. Everett died how much they cared about me as well. Mrs. Everett asked me to give the keynote speech for Dr. Everett at his funeral. It was a huge honor for me to do that.

SWIMMING WITH SHARKS

I have a recurring nightmare. I am outside some buildings alone. Classes are going on inside. I think I am supposed to be inside, but I can't face it. I have finished law school and don't know what to do. So I decide to go back and do it again. It was totally traumatic the first time, so I think, "How could I do that again? I must be crazy!"

The nightmare was so vivid that later in life I can recall every detail, even while wide awake. Must be some kind of post-traumatic stress disorder that still lingers.

In 1965 I was going to graduate from college at Yale. The war in Vietnam was going full blast and young men my age were coming home in body bags. I did not want to end up in a bag and did not know what to do. Flee to Canada? Pretend to be a pacifist? Join the Navy and hope to be sent to Italy? Continue on in graduate school and maintain my academic deferment? The options did not look good.

Tired of being stuck in New Haven and having scored less than the tippy top on my law boards, but needing to stay in school to avoid Vietnam, I applied to law school. The choice between dying in the Vietnam jungle and going to law school was a tough one. Neither option had much appeal, but I was having a long affair with a cute girl at Wellesley, a short motorcycle ride from Cambridge. So Harvard was my choice.

In those days, getting into law school was not about character or diversity. It was all about grades, law boards, and what elite undergraduate institution you had attended. I was a WASP and a total grade nerd from an elite college. Of course, I got accepted.

The Harvard version of law school lived up to my worst expectations. In those days it was a truly horrible place which perverted meritocracy and elitism into their most disgusting competitive forms. Harvard Law School back in the 1960s did not even try to make law an intellectually exciting or interesting subject. The whole idea was to create a highly trained combative lawyer, motivated only by money and devoid of ethical constraints, a warrior who could win any argument and write a brief for any side that would save the day for whatever corrupt criminal client could pay the hourly bill.

Most law students harbored no curiosity about the ethical or philosophical ambiguities of the legal conflicts they analyzed in class. They only wanted to convince the professor that they had the "right" answer. I found this to be intellectually disheartening.

I had additional problems with law school—two generic problems and one personal problem.

The first generic problem was unbridled, aggressive, ethics-free competition. Since lawyering is an adversarial game, there have to be winners and losers. Attackers and defenders. The classes at Harvard were intended to toughen up the students.

First-year students at Harvard Law in the late 1960s were treated to a level of classroom terror and abuse that would not be tolerated anywhere today. Nancy Boxley Tepper, one of the first women accepted at the law school, over the objections of the entire faculty, wrote in a magazine article years later that her worst nightmare was what the professors referred to as "Ladies Day."[17] On that day, she recalled, "each professor would call on a female student to recite and analyze the most embarrassing case he could find." Thirty years after graduating, she visited the classrooms and noticed the different, "relaxed" atmosphere. She asked the dean what was going on. He replied, "We discovered that students learn better when they are not scared witless all the time."

The second generic problem was what was euphemistically called the "Socratic Method" of teaching, otherwise known as the most ridiculous and impossible way to learn anything. Using this technique, professors would call on students in huge classrooms and try to humiliate them—make them appear to be complete fools. This was no easy feat because Harvard Law attracted some of the most arrogant and combative students in America. Even when a professor had reduced a student's pathetic argument to shreds, the typical aggressive student would persist in making a complete fool of himself.

---

[17] Nancy Boxley Tepper, "The Education of a Harvard Lawyer," *Harvard Magazine*, January-February 2021.

The classes were exercises in the Dunning-Kruger effect. Dunning and Kruger found in their extensive studies that those people who know the least believe that they know the most.[18] Each class I took at Harvard, before I quit attending classes altogether, was a sad regurgitation of the Dunning-Kruger experiments. The most arrogant and stubborn idiots would raise their hands and attempt to debate the professor, resulting in a lot of confusing classes in which clueless blowhards dominated a meaningless discussion from which nothing useful could be learned.

The first-year classroom situation at Harvard Law was so bizarre that one student, Scott Turow, wrote an entire book about the depraved cruelty and bullying involved. Later a movie, *The Paper Chase*, was made from that book. It portrayed in vivid detail the trauma and humiliation that Harvard Law students experienced in classes.

I could not bear to watch the film. Too close for comfort.

I was not alone in my revulsion to the system at Harvard Law School. In an extensive history of the school, *The Intellectual Sword: Harvard Law School, the Second Century*, the authors describe the school's "hyper-competitive student culture, [and] its confrontational pedagogy... an exacting, often brutal culture, which ground out lawyers by grinding down students. The culture's negative effects marked it as competitive to the point of being pathological." A faculty member told the authors, "Well, this is the unhappiest place." The authors point out that this kind of "education," if it can be called that, "helped shape a legendarily unhappy profession"—one that was home to "antisemitism, pro-Nazism, and spinelessness in the face of McCarthyism."

Apart from the brutality and other problems of the classroom culture, I had a personal problem. I could not afford to be there. I was living in abject poverty in a slum area, miles away, where you could rent a flat for less than half of the Cambridge prices. I had

---

[18] J. Kruger and D. Dunning, "Unskilled and unaware of it: How difficulties in recognizing one's own incompetence lead to inflated self-assessments," *Journal of Personality and Social Psychology* 77, no. 6 (1999): 1121-1134.

difficulty even physically getting to class. My transportation was an antique single-cycle BMW motorcycle. Getting from my ramshackle apartment to the law school and back on that bike in ice and snow was daunting. First of all, to keep from freezing, I had to wear about eight layers. When I showed up for class, I resembled a homeless person. That is probably one of the reasons that the professors always let me sit quietly in the back row and never harassed me with questions or asked me to move to my assigned seat.

As I recounted in another chapter, I eventually had an accident on the way to class, when a little old lady pulled out in front of me from a side street. I hit the brakes, the bike slid sideways into her car, and I went over her hood. I was unconscious for a while, and covered in blood and bruises. After a while, I was able to move the bike to the curb and walk to class, covered in dried blood. No one blinked an eye when I took my usual seat in the far back. The students were focused on confusing each other about the ancient English tort law cases that had been assigned, which, of course, I had not even read.

Between the transportation issues, my poverty, and the confusion generated in class by my Dunning-Kruger classmates, I realized that, despite playing the law-school game, I was getting nowhere. I really did not belong at Harvard Law School. Out of desperation and boredom, I quit going to classes and spent my time at home, in the library, and working. In the library I could ogle the cute girls who were always studying there, read the professors' law review articles on the class subjects, and score big points on the final exams by regurgitating the professors' own pet theories and opinions. By my second year, my grades, and, more important, my morale, improved dramatically. I was winning the game.

My situation was not unlike that which Richard Alpert wrote about in *Be Here Now*: "There was some point as a professor at Stanford and Harvard when I experienced being caught in some kind of meaningless game in which the students were exquisite at playing the role of students and the faculty were exquisite at playing the role of faculty. I would get up and say what I had read in books and they'd write it all down and give it back as answers on exams, but nothing was happening that mattered—that was real."

Of course, I was not the only student to realize that the outward law-school game was not the real game. I later learned that the top students had all figured out, long before I did, ways to game the game. Some of them would even cut key articles out of the law books at the library for their own use, depriving their classmates of the opportunity to read them. It was the Harvard way. Cut-throat.

When I was a freshman at Harvard, the most interesting news I heard on campus was about which of my classmates had attempted suicide and which ones had quit in disgust. This was a regular thing. I think the law school authorities took some perverted pride in the departure, dead or alive, of these less-than-maximum-warrior types. It was more proof that Harvard Law was a place only for the toughest of the tough.

Meanwhile, by 1966, the whole country was coming apart at the seams. Opposition to the Vietnam War was growing like wildfire. Sex, drugs, and rock and roll had captured an entire generation. I was not immune. Smoking joints in hippie pads and enjoying the pleasure of free love made it hard to stick with law school. It was another planet. I drifted mentally pretty far away, going to the school only to hit the library and show up for exams.

Oddly, because the Dunning-Kruger effect was so strong at Harvard, my distance from the classroom made it easier for me to understand the whole thing. I made it my job to determine what the professor wanted to hear. So I studied the professors' writings.

I had figured out how to handle the first two problems of law school, the ruthless competition and the Dunning-Kruger distractions. But I was still living in poverty. I did not have enough to eat or to buy gas for my motorcycle. I took on all kinds of part-time jobs in addition to my 20-hour-a-week scholarship job in the African Affairs Library. Temporary bartending jobs at special events got me good tips, especially if I added extra alcohol to the drinks. It was not uncommon to get a $50 tip now and then. That was enough to keep me going for a while. Moreover, there was food at the events—and leftovers to take home afterward.

When Michael Dukakis was running for office in Massachusetts, he hired me for his events. These were choice jobs because people at political fundraisers were rich, and Dukakis himself, although not rich, always gave me a huge tip.

The temp jobs were not enough. Then I found out that one could make big bucks giving blood. I went to all the hospitals as often as I could, way more times than technically allowable. Peter Bent Brigham Hospital paid $50 for a pint. The others offered less, but it added up. I finally ran out of blood. I was so weak that I could not have gone to class even if I wanted to.

Somehow, I survived three years of this misery. I found out after graduation that I had ended up with good grades. Who knew? Nevertheless, I was so bummed out by the law-school experience that I did not show up for graduation. I told them to send my diploma to my family's place in Maryland, where it probably ended up in the trash.

MARRIAGES AND DIVORCES

> *Lawyers believe a man is innocent until proven broke.*
> —attributed to Robin Hall

I have never been good at relationships, especially marriages. Growing up on a farm, the animals never rejected me. In high school, college and law school, I was always accepted. I was accepted in a fraternity. I was accepted in an exclusive senior society. It was all acceptance, acceptance, acceptance until I started having relationships with women and then marriages. Then it was all about rejection, rejection, rejection.

I was not the only one in my family to be bad at relationships. My father and mother had a tumultuous marriage, followed by a divorce that all of their children longed for. My two brothers have done better, only one divorce between them, but they made mistakes too. At least one of them did. He married a person who only wanted to argue and fight with him 24/7. He got divorced and is now trying to make it work with number two. My other brother is the only success story among the three of us brothers. But then, we always said he is a prince and a saint.

Both of my marriages started with a weird wedding and ended in divorce. I have never been good at the wedding part, and the divorce part has not been especially fun either. The part in between the wedding and the divorce seems to have been mostly about a failure to communicate. In my view, everything was poisoned by both the inauspicious weddings and the inevitable, looming divorces.

Some people have what they call good marriages. I don't know how they do it. I am not sure I believe them. I have had a few good days in my marriages, but the bad punctuation marks at the beginning and end and the rejection in the middle have just been miserable.

My first marriage, to Pippa Collingwood, was, in part at least, a "marriage of convenience." We were in our twenties and had spent quite a lot of time living and traveling together. She was a perfect travel companion, especially in Third World countries. (Our extensive travels are described in other stories in this book.) We got along well and had enjoyable times—epic adventures on some occasions, in fact. At home, Pippa was easygoing also. She made friends quickly and was an awesome cook, especially when it came to Turkish/Greek food.

Pippa was British, however, and when we got back to the U.S. after our long travels, she was on a 6-month tourist visa, and then an extension, and then another extension. Finally the immigration authorities said "enough already."

Our solution was to get married. Pippa did not much want to get married, especially to an American, a person from one of the colonies. She suggested that we move to the mother country, but I never found a job there, and I was not up for it anyway.

Pippa had been married before. She knew the score. Her first husband had left her on a farm he owned in Norfolk, East Anglia, to go live with his boyfriend in London. He was rich and bisexual, but apparently never helped Pippa out with expenses after he bolted. When I met her at the farm, she was throwing furniture into the fireplace to keep warm in the cold English winter. She subsisted on tea and crumpets. And my brother's chunk of Moroccan hash.

On the other hand, I was inexperienced with marriage, and saw no problem with the idea. Pippa could stay in America, we got along well, and we could continue having lots of fun as we had before being married. "What's the big deal with marriage anyway?" I thought.

While our wedding was not exactly a Downton Abbey type of affair, as my mother would have wished, it was a pretty mellow event. Only about 20 friends and relatives showed up. They were mostly well behaved.

The wedding was held outdoors at my mother's farm. My mother was ok with the plan because she liked Pippa. She liked her much more than my other friends, for several reasons. First of all, Pippa was well dressed, well spoken, intelligent, clean, and polite. She was not a degenerate drunkard or doper like some of the other people I associated with. Not only that, but mother learned that Pippa came from a "nice" family, which was always a key criterion for my mother. Pippa's father had served in the Royal Navy and had distinguished British Navy ancestors going way back. To top it off, they both loved nice things, like good china and silverware. The bottom line was that, in my mother's eyes, Pippa could do no wrong. It was definitely a good sign that the two of them got along so well. Life goes much smoother when your mother and the person you are living with are not at each other's throats.

There was one inauspicious thing about the wedding, however. I forgot to pay the minister who did the ceremony. I felt terrible about that oversight. I often wondered if he had put a curse on me or on our marriage because of that mistake.

I don't remember much about the party, but I do recall that some people stayed all night. One couple slept in a tent with campfires up in the orchard. Another group took up quarters in the hay barn. I was pretty sure they would burn it to the ground, smoking their joints, but somehow we got lucky, and that didn't happen, at least not that night. Sadly, someone did burn the barn completely to the ground a few years later. It was one hell of a bonfire.

After a few years of living in Washington, D.C., Pippa took off to Barbados with a girlfriend from England. Eventually she went back to London on her own. I was saddened, but not terribly surprised. It was never a real marriage in the normal sense. We got along well. We had great trips and lots of fun together, but she didn't want to live in the U.S. long term. Pippa thought the whole country was a nut house, a looney bin, and it is hard to argue with that assessment. Americans had normalized a lot of craziness, even before the extreme polarization of the MAGA era. While I was not happy to see her leave, the good times we had enjoyed together made for some interesting stories, some of which are in this book.

When I decided I needed a divorce from Pippa so that I could get rejected by someone new, I wrote to her in London and asked her for her consent. She wrote back something to the effect of: "You can do whatever you want if you send me the shoes that I left in the closet." She added some sarcastic advice, saying that I was probably going to marry some American bimbo, and that I could obviously make whatever stupid mistakes I wanted, as I usually did. (She predicted that one with uncanny accuracy.)

I sent the shoes to her, and showed her letter to the judge at the divorce hearing. The judge looked at her letter and said: "That looks like consent to me. Divorce granted."

I thought at the time, "Well. Marriage and divorce are not such a big deal."

Big mistake.

My second marriage was to a completely different kind of person. I will just use her initial: G. She was quite beautiful. In fact she had won a beauty contest in high school. People still remark to me 40 years later about how attractive she was when she was young. Somehow I deluded myself into thinking we got along well, and at least she was not a degenerate, dope-smoking hippie like some of my other girlfriends at the time.

Of course, I needed to meet my future wife's parents. Up to the New Jersey coast we went. My bride-to-be was a Jersey girl, born and bred from an Italian family. Her grandmother never spoke a word of English, but her dad was a successful second-generation Italian.

I knew right away that it was going to be an interesting family when we drove into the entrance of her dad's house on the water. Featured prominently in the front yard was a plaster statue of the Virgin Mary, with an outboard motor under repair propped up against it. A bicycle tube was hung over Mary's head. They were supposedly devout Catholics, but the kind from southern Italy, which apparently is a lot like the Southern Appalachians. The rest of the front yard was populated with surf boards, marine equipment, and car parts. The house itself was a modest shore place, but chaos reigned inside.

G.'s mother greeted me, sort of. She was a large woman, quite intimidating, with a strange wig. The wig was on backwards. She talked through the hair. A little later, I learned that she was mentally ill and taking lots of medication that rendered her significantly disoriented.

Eventually my future father-in-law, Paul, showed up after driving in from his office. He was a very sweet man. He had raised three strong-willed daughters with a mentally ill wife, so he was a bit beaten down, but he was always generous and friendly. He was popular with everyone.

We sat down to dinner.

If you have ever eaten dinner in a real honest-to-goodness southern Italian household, you might be prepared for this meal. I was not. Piles of spaghetti and bread, as well as manicotti and other foods, were scattered around the table. Wine was in big gallon jugs. Everyone was grabbing whatever they could. It was tons of fun.

Paul drank wine out of a large water glass. I asked him about wine glasses. He said, "We don't do that French stuff." After that, I quit drinking wine out of wine glasses myself. Too small and too fragile.

They would never survive a genuine Italian dinner. When people give me grief about not using wine glasses even today, I say, "My Italian father-in-law taught me about wine glasses. Italians don't use them, so neither do I."

I really loved Paul. Everyone did, but the rest of the family was harder to like. When Paul died years later, the two older sisters kicked out his girlfriend who had been taking care of him, tore the place up, and cleaned out his bank account, giving their younger sister, G., nothing. G. was shocked.

Our wedding raised some doubts as to how things would go afterwards. Overtly it seemed fairly standard. It was in a church in New Jersey. I invited no one from my family because I realized that my mother, expecting a Downton Abbey scene, would not get along well with the distinctly not-very-posh family I was marrying into. She was pissed about not being invited, but it needed to be that way.

Just before the ceremony I found myself momentarily alone in the parking lot. G.'s family and friends were inside the church. I thought to myself, "I can still make a run for it. There is still time. This time, the whole marriage thing does not sound like fun. I could just bolt across this parking lot and never be seen again." I still think that would have been my best move, but I chickened out.

In my own delusional way, I thought, "What the hell? If it doesn't work out, I can give her some shoes back and forget about the whole thing."

G. and I had a roughly conventional life for two decades, but in reality it was two separate lives. She was practicing yoga continuously, and teaching it as well. I was working long hours and then going kayaking every spare minute I had. We did not share much, but we managed to produce three children.

On the back end of every bad marriage, of course, is the rejection and then, finally, the divorce.

My divorce this time was radically different from the first. Very harsh. G. was bitter about my frequent absences from the home front, when I was off kayaking in Alaska and Chile and places like that while she was managing the house and three children.

G. claimed to be able to see people's auras. She told me that I had the aura of a snake. It was a black aura, she said. When I heard that, I knew it was "game over."

The divorce was a sad, costly, mean-spirited war. Scorched earth. No fun at all. We fought over everything. We both had lawyers who intended to take home for themselves every asset the family had. My first lawyer was so aggressive that I once told him to take it easy and that I did not want to win if it meant the loss of everything and the total destruction of the family. He took offense at that and immediately fired me as his client. My second lawyer was more of a conciliatory type, but like all divorce lawyers, the game was to make as much money as you can off the whole miserable process. My wife's lawyer was a total take-no-prisoners killer who wanted me to be left broke or dead. Preferably both.

The divorce battle ruined both of our lives and badly damaged our youngest children. One younger child survived more or less intact, but one did not. My son was close to his mother. When she left, he attempted suicide. (More about that in a later story.) I did not understand what was happening with him and was not able to help him much, although I loved him dearly. His mental condition continued to deteriorate. I rarely see him, and this makes me miserable.

When we finally got to court, many thousands of dollars of legal fees later, the four-time-divorced lady judge started with a question for me. "What was the date of your marriage?" I said, "I don't remember. I will have to look that up for you." She said, "Well, I guess that's why you're here, Mr. Barrow." It went downhill rapidly from there. I ended up with my pension destroyed, my house gone, sleeping in the back seat of my car with only partial custody of one child.

The lawyers won that battle. Totally.

My divorce seemed harsh to me, but then I had nothing similar to compare it to. Then I got a call from my lawyer. She wanted me to come get all my papers. She was closing her office and quitting the practice of divorce law forever. She said that our case had finished her off. Even secondhand, the emotional and psychological toll was just too much for her. The raw cruelty and hatred she had to endure to get through our case was more then she could handle ever again, she said. This was after 35 years of divorce practice. That gave me some perspective.

I was not the only one in my immediate family to have weddings that either went off the rails or almost did. My brother Henry had an inauspicious wedding experience his first time around. The wedding itself was more or less survivable. In fact it was fun. But the preliminary events were nothing short of world-class scandalous. First there was the bachelor's party, which my brothers and I agreed to arrange. This was an event that never should have been conceived, never should have been planned, and never should have occurred. It got out of control.

For the bachelor's party, we'd borrowed the use of a large house owned by a friend of one of my brothers. It was in Cleveland Park, a nice northwest D.C. neighborhood. The owners of that house will never again loan out their house to anyone. The damage was extensive. The menu was piles of cocaine, alcohol, alcohol, and more alcohol. Every male person we knew was invited.

I was assigned the task of finding the entertainment. What do I know about entertainment? Not much. So I turned to one of my more worldly friends, a person whose name I am forbidden to mention in this book. In short order, this worldly experienced individual procured a team of "ladies" who promised to give everyone a "really good time." My dad was invited, and they gave him a very good time first, before attending to everyone else at the party who was interested. I think my dad was a bit shell-shocked by the experience. I think he considered things a bit too decadent. But at least he was happy to have been invited.

The wedding was the next day. Some people, including my youngest brother, Jake, failed to make an appearance at the actual wedding, having endured so much of one vice or another at the previous day's event. Jake was still comatose on a pool table in the borrowed house when he was finally roused by a cleaning lady.

Henry's wedding was a simple affair, followed by an event which made us all see the world differently. I gave the happy couple a wedding gift of a balloon ride across the countryside in Howard County, Maryland, where our farm was located. Even our mother got in the gondola, the passenger basket below the balloon. It was fabulous. A good omen—but the marriage was doomed anyway.

My dad's second wedding was another one that went a bit off the rails. He was marrying a Mormon teetotaler, so my brothers and I made an effort to ensure that he had enough alcohol before the wedding to last him for his entire marriage. Most of the drinks were consumed before and at the pre-wedding dinner. Dad distinguished himself at the pre-wedding dinner by grabbing the waitress by her rear end and complimenting her on her front bumpers. All this was in front of his wife-to-be and her son, a Mormon minister who was to oversee the wedding the next day.

All I can say about that is that the wedding the next day was a little tense.

After this experience, my dad's new wife, Dorothy, banned him from ever touching alcohol again. He cooperated for a while until I went to visit the happy couple in North Carolina about a year later and took him a bottle of single malt scotch. He and I stayed up all night telling stories and finishing off the bottle. The next day Dorothy said to me that it was time for me to leave because I had undone 14 months of hard work on her part to wean him off the bottle.

Sorry, Dorothy.

FROG-WALKED OUT OF THE WHITE HOUSE

There was a small crowd gathering in the West Wing of the White House. I was there for a signing ceremony, for a bill which I had worked on for about three years in my job as a Congressional staff person.

Suddenly there was a kerfuffle of some kind near the door. We all looked over. Four burly Secret Service guys with earphones were asking questions of people near the door. They seemed to be looking for someone. And in a hurry.

Within a few seconds some of the crowd began pointing in the direction where I was standing. The Secret Service guys took off quickly towards the area where I was standing. They were looking straight at me. "Oh my God!" I thought. "They are coming for me! What did I do?"

I was excited to be at the White House. It isn't every day that a Congressional staff person is invited to this kind of big political event. But this development was a little too exciting. My heart was beating like a jackhammer.

All the Senators and Members of Congress and staff people who had even the slightest thing to do with the passage of this particular bill were there in front, awaiting the entrance of the President.

Panic set in. "What should I do?" I thought about running for it, but there was nowhere to run. Nowhere to hide. I could not imagine what they had found out about me that would cause such an emergency.

They quickly got to me, all four of them. I raised my hands and said, "I am not armed. I didn't do anything. You got the wrong guy."

One Secret Service guy with wires and things stuck in his ear said: "We got the right guy. Come with us, sir. Right now!"

All four of them gathered around me and frog-walked me out of the room. Everyone was looking at me and mumbling to each other. They all probably suspected that I was involved in something very big, something very bad. It was embarrassing. And scary.

After they had escorted me safely off the White House premises, one of them said "You need to go to 4th and Constitution right now. The police will be waiting." Without saying more, they turned away quickly and left me standing on the sidewalk outside the fence. Baffled.

"What could possibly have happened? Why was I perp-walked out of the White House, deposited on the sidewalk, and told nothing?"

I caught a cab to the location they specified. Still mystified.

When I got to 4th and Constitution, I found my car parked on the corner facing the wrong way on a one-way street. My wife was standing on the sidewalk with my one-year-old daughter, Isabel, and a big D.C. motorcycle cop looking irritated.

"What's going on? What happened?" I asked. The cop responded, "This lady made a wrong turn into a one-way street, and she has no license or registration. We contacted your office and told them to get you here immediately to straighten this out."

"Oh God!" I said. "I was just at the White House for a special occasion. Couldn't this wait?"

The cop was totally unimpressed and probably did not believe me anyway.

I started to negotiate with him. "Nobody was hurt. Nothing was damaged," I pleaded.

He was not up for negotiation. He began writing a ticket.

Meanwhile, my little daughter Isabel was freaked out and getting more and more upset. She was standing next to a big scary jack-booted motorcycle cop while her father was saying things she did not understand. Suddenly she let loose. She was not wearing a diaper and the pee poured out. Most of it splashed onto the officer's polished boot.

The cop was not pleased. I am sure he wanted to add another ticket to the first one for the offense of pissing on an officer of the law. I doubt that that particular act was specified in the D.C. Criminal Code.

Suddenly, the cop wanted to get the hell out of there. He threw the ticket at me, fired up his motorcycle, and raced off in a cloud of exhaust.

I was quite proud of Isabel. I would have done the same thing she did if I thought I could get away with it.

A VERY BAD DAY

"Did you know Scott Coulter died?" I asked my friend Mac Thornton on the phone.

"Yeah. I know. It wasn't the virus. He had pancreatic cancer, but he beat it, so that was not it. He fell off his roof."

"Jesus!" I said.

"Well, I guess that's a better way to go than the virus. Or pancreatic cancer."

"Yeah. At least it's quick. You have a few seconds to look down, and then, boom! It's over."

Better, I thought, than being thrown in one of those refrigerator trucks they used during the pandemic to store the overflow of dead bodies outside hospitals. People who suffocated because they couldn't breathe anymore, even with tubes stuck down their throats.

"Scott was a great guy," I said. "He had a huge laugh. He was fun to hang around with. He had a company he called 'Destruction Construction.' He once told me, 'I am not so great at construction, but I am hell on wheels when it comes to the destruction stuff.' I hired him to tear out my basement back then. Did a great job."

"Ed Grove died, too. Did you know that?" Mac said. "He had some adopted kids. He came home one day and one of them had shot himself in the living room. I don't think that had anything to do with his own death, but . . ."

I didn't say anything. But something awful came instantly to mind.

I came home one day, many years ago, to hear a strange thumping sound upstairs. I went up and found my teenage son banging his wrists against the wall in his bedroom. He wanted to get more blood out. He had cut both of his wrists. He was banging his hands on the wall because he was not bleeding out as fast as he wanted.

There was a weird smell that I had never smelled before. Human blood. Lots of it. Covering the walls of his bedroom.

I called 911 and grabbed my 4-year-old daughter to take her to the hospital with us when the ambulance arrived. It was the worst day of my life, by far.

Waiting on the front stairs, I tried to talk to my son, but he was not making much sense. He had been drinking a lot. I told him we all loved him and needed him to live.

He was diagnosed as a schizophrenic, whatever that means. I have never been more saddened by anything in my life.

10

THE COMEDIES OF OLD AGE

THE COOKIE MONSTER

> *Umbrage transitus est tempos nostrum.*
> —Latin for "our lives are short"

My mother loved chocolate chip cookies. When she got old and developed Parkinson's disease, plus dementia, the attraction to chocolate chip cookies only got stronger.

Often she would ask one of her three sons to take her to the store to get groceries, usually only chocolate chip cookies and a stack of frozen Swanson TV dinners. She would eat both on a TV tray in front of the TV.

While devouring the gourmet dinner, she would invariably be watching a show involving a risk-taking Australian outdoorsman who wandered around in the outback wrestling with crocodiles, fighting off killer spiders, and facing down huge poisonous snakes. He did all kinds of dangerous things and finally died from one of his adventures offshore. A big stingray stabbed him in the stomach with its barbed tail.

Mother was fascinated by that show. She watched the reruns over and over. She would shake her head in amazement as he grabbed a poisonous snake or faced down another dangerous creature in the outback. Turning to me, she would say, "Can you believe that! That guy is crazy!"

The trips to the grocery store were traumatic for those of us who drove her. We would sometimes lose track of her in the store. Invariably, we would find her in the cookie aisle, standing there munching cookies. Crumbs and torn cookie boxes all over the floor.

I would scold her. "Mother, you can't just open and eat those in the store. You have to pay for them first."

Her answer was always the same. "Why? They have lots of them here, all stacked up."

The logic of this was not clear to me, but it made sense to her.

It was a big mistake for her to try driving on her own. She was a real danger to everything on the road and shopping area even before she got into the store. Her parking technique was pure bumper car. Her car was crumpled with thousands of dents from hitting other cars in the parking lot.

Even before my mother got old and confused, she was a terrible driver. When I was about 4 years old, she parked her car on a steep hill in Ellicott City, Maryland, while she ran into a store, leaving me in the car. The car started rolling down the hill. That story is told in an earlier chapter.

On another occasion, during a huge rainstorm, she decided to drive across the low bridge on Old Fredrick Road next to our farm. The stream was flooded with rising water. She did not make it across. She had to climb out of the window and swim to land.

By the time she was getting up in age and progressing with Parkinson's disease, she became an even worse driver. She was also not particularly adept at getting from the store to the parking lot with a grocery bag. Once, unknown to the family, she exited from Kmart (her favorite store), stepped off the curb in front of a delivery van, and got wiped out. Many bones broken. She was carted off to the hospital by ambulance.

A few day after her disappearance, I got worried and called the police. They went on a missing-person search and finally located her in St. Agnes hospital south of Baltimore. When hospital authorities had asked her who they should contact, she had replied, "No one. They are all traveling in Europe." Of course no one was in Europe, but she knew we were all going to give her hell about going to Kmart on her own and walking in and out without a cane or walker. She did not want to hear it.

I went over to the hospital and read her the Riot Act. She was all wrapped up head to toe in bandages, with her broken leg in a big sling. "Why didn't you call me or someone? We were worried to death."

"Well. I didn't want to worry you boys."

That logic escaped me also. She had her own logic by this time.

Even in her most demented stage of life, she was not completely without guile, however. When we took her car keys away to save her life and the lives of everyone else on the road, she defeated us. Secretly, she called the car dealer and had him quietly bring her a new set of keys.

And off she went.

WHEN EVERYTHING GETS OLD

> *I'm at the age where food has taken the place of sex in my life. In fact, I have just had a mirror put over my kitchen table.*
> —attributed to Rodney Dangerfield

This essay is an expanded version of a note I wrote for inclusion in my annual high-school alumni publication. It was rejected. The editor said, "It's too depressing. Can't you rewrite it to tell about how happy you are at age 79? Your classmates don't want to be reminded of all the miserable stuff you wrote."

Until recently, I have always been drawn to old things. My last car was a 1997 jalopy. I live in a 125-year-old house in a so-called "historic" neighborhood. "Historic," I have finally realized, is a euphemism for dilapidated. The house is falling down, like every other house in the historic neighborhood. Every day, I plan another project to keep it going, but as time goes on, I am losing that battle. When entropy blends with procrastination, the results are not good.

Apart from an old car and a deteriorating home, I have also had two ancient boats and am part owner of a 200-plus-year-old farm. I am also losing the battles with those. The current boat is degenerating into fiberglass wreckage as I watch listlessly. The farm I also ignore as it slowly rots away, returning to nature.

Then there is my body. It is also not acting fabulously youthful. It has issues, metastatic prostate cancer being the most debilitating. It spread to spine, hips, lymph nodes, and who knows where else, and is probably going to finish me off before this book gets printed. It is currently dormant, but I have six doctors and take seven drugs a day to keep my old corpse staggering around. The details of that experience are revealed in a later story.

I am starting to think that maybe "old" is not what it is cracked up to be. My kids probably have the undertaker on speed dial.

Most of what "experts" have written about growing old is contained in alarming books like *The Dark Flood Rises*, *Losing it: In Which an Aging Professor Laments His Shrinking Brain*, or *Why I Hope I Die at 75*.

Yikes!

On the brighter side, I try to keep from free-falling through all this deterioration. I went to New Orleans for Mardi Gras to perk myself up. That was a mistake, though; it was just too crazy for an old-timer like me. I came home early, before the truly wacko stuff got underway. I play pickleball every other day with six young girls. They are all over 70, but still much younger than me. Like me, most of them have their aged bodies duct-taped together in various ways. But we all hit the ball around, having fun, pretending that we are still real athletes.

Also on an upbeat note, in 2019 before the Age of the Virus, my partner, Amber, and I went to France with another couple and drove a little rented canal boat along the beautiful rivers and canals of Burgundy. Only a few locks were damaged by our limited boating skills. Lots of wine and good French food ashore along the way. Not too strenuous. No terrible mistakes.

Another thrill for me is having grandkids. One of them is a 10-year-old hockey player. I love to watch him play Sunday mornings during the season. His whole team can skate better than I ever could. They are amazing.

THE EMPEROR OF ALL MALADIES

In my 60s, a dread disease showed up in my annual blood test. My family doc found that I had an elevated Prostate-Specific Antigen (PSA) level. When that happens, it usually means cancer of the prostate.

Off to the Brady Clinic (named after a hospital benefactor known as Diamond Jim Brady) I went. The clinic specializes in prostate cancer. It is part of the Johns Hopkins Hospital in Baltimore. Hopkins is supposedly one of the three or four best places in the world to have prostate cancer dealt with. (But who knows for sure?) A scan showed cancer in my prostate.

"Darn!" I thought. "My luck has finally run out. This is not going to be fun. The good times are over."

But not so fast. There are now various treatments for prostate cancer: radiation with an external beam, insertion of radioactive "seeds" in the prostate, and surgery to remove the whole gland (prostectomy). All have benefits and drawbacks. Not liking the presence of a deadly cancer in my body, I opted for surgery.

Dr. Misop Han at the Brady Clinic was an expert in the use of robotic laparoscopic surgery for prostate cancer. He had practiced extensively on rats and mice, he told me, before using the big million-dollar machine on humans. Into the surgery I went. Never saw Dr. Han. He was on a computer screen in another room.

As I lay on the hospital gurney, scared out of my wits, a huge machine with bulging camera eyes and long arms with multiple complex metal joints loomed over me. "This is not going to end well," I thought. I greeted the huge alien monster with a faint "Hello."

No answer. I was alone with this thing. It seemed more like a space creature than a medical device.

Soon the anesthesia had me out cold. I woke up several hours later, feeling weak and nauseated, with two small holes in my abdomen. I could not control my urine at first and had to wear diapers for weeks and weeks.

Recovery was slow. The operation had taken a lot of my energy and strength. But Dr. Han announced that "We got it all out. You are good to go. Come back for a checkup in a month."

I felt relieved. I thought that my ordeal was over.

Not so.

Cancer was labeled "The Emperor of All Maladies" by the physician and science writer Siddhartha Mukherjee—because it is smart, tricky, and powerful. Mine had sneaked out of the prostate before the operation and, within a decade, had metastasized all over my body. It was out to kill me. "My luck has now run out for sure," I thought.

I called Dr. Han. He was not encouraging.

I said, "I thought you said I was good to go?"

"You are never in the clear with prostate cancer," he said.

This was news to me. And not good news.

Off I went to Georgetown Hospital's Lombardi Cancer Center to see what they could do. By this time, I was pretty well convinced that I was not long for this world. I met up with Dr. Nancy Dawson, who specializes in metastatic prostate cancer, and she took me on as a patient. She started me out on androgen deprivation injections and then added a newer oral medication called Zytiga, all designed to wipe out my testosterone. Apparently, prostate cancer considers testosterone to be like candy. It thrives on it. So, if you get rid of the testosterone, the theory goes, the cancer might go away or at least slow down.

As so often happens with me, Lady Luck was on my side. The treatment worked. My PSA plummeted. By 2022, my PSA remained low, and the scans could no longer find any cancer nodes. I went off the drugs. As this book goes to press, the doctors are scratching their heads and searching for answers: "Where did the cancer go? Is it really gone, or just hiding again?"

MY LAST BIG ADVENTURE

> *For many elderly Americans old age is a tragedy, a period of quiet despair, deprivation, desolation and muted rage.*
> –Robert Neil Butler, *Why Survive? Being Old in America*, 1975

I have had a few big adventures over the years. Sailing the ocean and numerous seas. A shipwreck offshore. Kayaking waterfalls in Chile. Traveling from London to Kathmandu overland in a $200 van. Hitchhiking through North Africa. Kayaking Desolation Sound. Living in the Amazon jungle. Racing schooners through storms. It's an eclectic list.

My next big adventure looks like it's going to be the last, a meet-up with the Grim Reaper (I refer to her as "G.R."). So far, a team of skilled doctors at Johns Hopkins, Dana Farber, and Georgetown have kept G.R. on the front porch. But chances are, she is eventually going to sneak in to give me the final whack. Unless I manage to kill myself ahead of time trying to have too much fun.

If you have read this far in this memoir, it is pretty obvious by now that my closing act may well be the result of a careless accident arising out of a misguided attempt to have a good time—which I will fail to survive.

The Rolling Stone gonzo journalist, Hunter Thompson, declared: "Life should not be a journey to the grave with the intention of arriving safely in a pretty and well-preserved body, but rather to skid in broadside in a cloud of smoke, thoroughly used up, totally worn out, and loudly proclaiming 'Wow! What a ride!'" Thompson was 67 when he skidded in broadside with a bullet in his head. He tried to stir up some more smoke afterward by having Johnny Depp shoot his ashes into the sky with a cannon.

My partner Amber's mother took the opposite approach. A God-fearing Christian, she favored dragging her final act out endlessly. She issued instructions to the doctors and her family to keep her alive by any means as long as medically possible. The long miserable journey to her final end was a marvel of medical science, but it was, nevertheless, an ugly, painful trip to the finish line.

So . . . what's my plan?

I am well past the age for skidding into anything in a cloud of smoke, but I am definitely not in the dragging-it-out school either.

At this point, my exit strategy is a work in progress. I hope to crack a few jokes, keep the pain meds coming, maybe eat a few more magic mushrooms, avoid too much drama, and try to have as much fun as I can until the music stops.

I feel fortunate that I discarded religion a good while ago, so I don't have to seek forgiveness for my misdeeds. What a relief! Having escaped the ugly trap of religion, I don't have to fret about heaven or hell. Fearing God's wrath and all that.

My dad always said that it was important to have fun. I took him seriously. It seems that one cannot always have fun without some risk. Having fun often involves some serious mishaps, such as the one described in the story entitled "We Were Damn Lucky."

Working with my dad's concept, when I arrived at Yale, I thought that my mission there was to have fun. I was not, it is safe to say, the most mature undergrad at Yale, but I did have fun for all four years, inside and outside the classroom.

After a not-so-fun intermission in law school, I resumed the mission of finding fun. First, I went to work in the circus, a.k.a. the House of Representatives. My task there was to try to put into logical English the strange and often incoherent ideas that members of Congress thought up in their most delusional moments. It was a peculiar task, but often an enjoyable one.

I wanted even more exotic fun, however. It was the hippie era, and the hippies were clearly having all the fun: free love, drugs, music, wild times. I quit my job to join them. After the mandatory Woodstock trip, I took the hippie trail from London to Kathmandu by land, over mostly dirt roads in a cheap van. Hitchhiking through North Africa. The opportunities for finding fun in the exotic hippie travel zones were plentiful. Peace and love, brother. But you did have to throw caution to the wind and trust that some of substances you were imbibing would not blow off the top of your head.

After the hippie dream burned out, I became obsessed with the exciting sport of kayaking and surfing on whitewater rivers, even jumping off waterfalls for an extra thrill. As recounted in this book, I travelled all over, as far as Patagonia, to find the best whitewater. That took years, because the world is filled with intoxicating rivers and waterfalls.

When I started to age out of the kayaking scene, I fell for the exceedingly fun sports of windsurfing, kiteboarding, and especially sailing. I sailed across the Atlantic Ocean. Circumnavigated Vancouver Island. Raced schooners through storms. Sailed through the Bahamas several times and checked out a variety of other Caribbean islands

Sailboats, however, can break down, have accidents, and even sink, in inconvenient places at inconvenient times. Not so much fun. But then . . . you can have the exquisite experience of getting yourself out of trouble. As recounted earlier, I once experienced the total loss of my father's boat miles offshore in the Atlantic Ocean in a nasty storm. The storm blew me ashore like a piece of flotsam. The boat went to the bottom, thankfully without me in it. There is nothing more exhilarating than crawling up on a safe beach after something like that.

Later in life, I learned to dance to zydeco music and had way too much fun in southwest Louisiana and elsewhere, dancing to the intoxicating beat of musicians like Boozoo Chavis, Roy Carrier, and Beau Jocque, sometimes in dilapidated clubs on the banks of alligator-infested bayous. Loads of fun.

Now there is the question of getting old. Can you still have fun as age takes its toll? That's the challenge I am currently working on. It cannot continue to be the strenuous, physical, outdoor activities I used to enjoy. My body refuses to cooperate. But lots of fun is still to be had, especially if you are as delusional as I am about age. I continue enjoying music and beautiful things; also learning new things. Then there is playing pickleball with other old timers, and lazy afternoons across a backgammon table. A canal trip with friends in France is not bad, either.

I am not going to go out in complete accord with Hunter Thompson's concept of the thrilling gonzo death, but I do intend to keep the fun meter as far up in the red zone as I can, right up until I croak.

My fun meter

When I get off the train, wherever my ashes get blown to, I hope everybody they land on will be having as much fun as I did.

> *All messed up with nowhere to go*
> *I stare at myself in the mirror alone*
> *It's hard to make friends when you're half in the grave*
> *But I ain't dead yet.*
>
> –Lord Huron, "Not Dead Yet," 2021

EPILOGUE

MEMORY, TRUTH, FICTION, AND REALITY

We're all sitting on top of a slippery mess of memories, and no matter how true *they are, they're real in the sense that there's some reason that they're there. More than anything, maybe, they tell us about who we are.*
—Elizabeth Strout, quoted in Joe Fassler, "When Memories Are True Even When They're Not," *The Atlantic*, May 2, 2017

All this happened, more or less.
—Kurt Vonnegut, *Slaughterhouse-Five*, 1969

No one should trust their memories, nor anyone else's memories.

In my mind, the stories in this collection are all more or less true, with some editing to protect the innocent. I think that the events happened as I remember them. Obviously, that is delusional. We all think of memories as videos in our brains—but that is not the case. Anything we think we remember may be partly or even entirely fictional. And this gets worse with age. As memories fade, they are replaced in part by imagination and confabulation.

People who have heard or read the stories in this book often ask me, "Did that really happen?"

Or, "Is that true, or are you making it up?"

Those are good questions. Any memoir is a collection of stories based only on memory. Even if the author is trying his or her best to be accurate and truthful, memories are suspect.

In some of the stories in this collection, I have asked other people who were there at the time of the events described to tell me their version of the events. I thought that maybe their version would provide me with what Oliver Sacks calls "a corrective to the deceits of memory and fantasy."[19]

Naturally, their memories differed radically from mine. I considered their responses, and considered what the actor Christopher Walken said in an interview: "The truth is good, but interesting is better."[20] I began to feel like Blanche DuBois in *A Streetcar Named Desire* when she exclaimed: "I don't want realism. I want magic. . . . I don't tell the truth. I tell what *ought* to be the truth."[21]

With memory, there are several problems that I've discovered. First, flawed perception. Second, flawed recall. Then there is the postmodern philosophical denial of objective truth, and, finally, the troubling questions about reality itself raised by quantum mechanics and psychedelic experiences.

UNRELIABLE PERCEPTIONS

Even before we try to remember something, we perceive what is going on. Unfortunately, what we see, hear, smell, and touch is faulty. Our perceptions are selective. Ask any magician. Magicians make their living by making you think you are seeing and hearing something that is not there, or not seeing and hearing something that is there. They make a living out of manipulating our perceptions. According

---

[19] Oliver Sacks, *On the Move: A Life* (Knopf, 2015), 384.
[20] Quoted in David Marchese, "Christopher Walken Shares the Secrets of Acting Like Christopher Walken," *The New York Times*, February 8, 2022.
[21] Tennessee Williams, *A Streetcar Named Desire,* premiered 1947.

to magicians, it's a matter of attention. If they can change what you are paying attention to, they can change your reality.[22]

The psychologist Richard Gregory argues that human perceptions are not just "simple reproductions of sensory data from the eye or ear," but have to be "constructed by the brain."[23]

Cognitive scientists such as Julia Shaw, author of *The Memory Illusion*, have proved that, even in the absence of outside manipulation, our own brains manipulate our perceptions by picking and choosing what we need to see in any particular scene. That selectivity of perception was developed in our brains over thousands of years of evolution as a survival mechanism. Don't look at the trees and flowers when a saber-tooth tiger is sneaking up on you. We see and hear only what the model of the universe in our brain allows us to see and hear. Maria Konnikova explains in her wonderful book *The Confidence Game*: "We don't see objectively. We see the version [of events] that best suits our desires."

David Brooks explained in a *New York Times* article: "Much or most of seeing is making mental predictions about what you expect to see, based on experience, and then using sensory input to check and adjust your predictions."[24]

According to cognitive scientist Terry Allard, "Humans travel around in their own model of the world and we search for information that confirms what our internal models tell us should be there."[25] Ed

---

[22] Magic allows us to indulge in "the human desire to be fooled—to slip the cuffs of reality and believe, if only briefly, the unbelievable." Dan Barry, "The Curious, Astounding Collection of the Magician Ricky Jay," *The New York Times*, Oct 19, 2021.

[23] Richard Gregory, *Concepts and Mechanisms of Perception* (London: Duckworth, 1974).

[24] David Brooks, "You Are Not Who You Think You Are," *The New York Times*, September 2, 2021.

[25] Terry Allard, Ph.D., personal interview, 2022. Dr. Allard received his Ph.D. from the Massachusetts Institute of Technology in Psychology and Brain Science (1984) and post-doctoral training in neurophysiology and animal behavior at the University of California.

Catullus of Pixar Animation Studios says: "We only see 40 percent of reality with our eyes. The rest is filled in by our brain."[26]

Not only is every individual's perception of an event flawed to begin with, but everyone else's memory of the same event is also flawed and likely to be different. According to psychologists, "When two people produce entirely different accounts of the same event, observers usually assume that one of them is lying."[27] Eyewitness accounts are notoriously unreliable.

My partner, Amber, and I once went to the Arena Stage in Washington, D.C., to watch a comedy/magic show.

We had been watching the two magicians pull off some pretty wild stunts, and we were enjoying the show. When one of them asked for a volunteer for another illusion, I raised my hand and pointed to Amber, sitting next to me. They called her to come up on stage. To my amazement, she got out of her seat and went up. I still wonder why.

Amber is fearful of EVERYTHING. When she gets up in the morning, she checks the local news to see how many killings, muggings, and carjackings have occurred in our vicinity in the past 24 hours. (Quite a few, sometimes.) She issues warnings to me no matter what I go out to do: "Be careful! Don't take any chances. Don't fall off your bicycle. Keep your Covid mask on." Etc., etc.

Amber's fears developed out of growing up in a crime-ridden part of Detroit and then going to college in the Detroit ghetto where, she recalls vividly, getting raped and robbed on campus was as common as getting a milkshake.

I will never understand why Amber decided to go on stage and get herself chopped into pieces by two clowns. It seemed so out of character.

What I was looking at from my seat in the second row did not look all that funny. One part of my mind said to the other part: "It's

---

[26] Quoted in Joshua Jay, *How Magicians Think: Misdirection, Deception, and Why Magic Matters* (Workman Publishing, 2021), 308.

[27] Carol Travis and Elliot Aronson, *Mistakes Were Made (But Not By Me)* (Harcourt, 2007), 69.

just a trick. Be cool." The other part said to the first part: "What if something goes wrong? Accidents happen sometimes in these shows. That saw does not look healthy."

Amber was lying down on her back in a long, brightly painted box. There appeared to be blood stains (red paint?) staining the middle of the box. Amber's head poked out one end. Her feet stuck out the other end. She looked apprehensive. One magician was bent down, talking to her, trying to reassure her and keep her laughing. His partner was waving around a big ugly saw. He announced to the audience, "Don't worry. I have done this successfully once before in rehearsal."

When the magician-clowns rolled out the box and brandished the saw, I suspected that Amber was probably thinking about bolting off the stage. She glanced at me with a look that said, "Get me out of here!" But they coaxed her to lie more or less still.

I felt helpless. I knew, of course, that it was a trick, but it still made me uneasy. What if Amber got so scared that she moved around, or tried to get out, and screwed up the trick?

The show proceeded. While one of the clowns talked nonstop to Amber, face-to-face, the other talked nonstop to the audience and started to saw the box in half. The audience gasped. We were all a little on edge as he struggled clumsily with the big saw. Part of the act, or not? When he finished sawing through the entire box, there was silence in the theater. Amber looked comatose. The clowns then pulled both sides of the box apart, with Amber now separated into two parts.

Everyone clapped. Except me. I started to rise out of my seat when . . .

. . . the clowns pushed the two halves of the box back together, and Amber climbed out, unharmed.

Neither of us knows, to this day, how that trick was done, but now we go to every magic show we can find. Amber tries to figure out how each illusion is performed. I sit in silence and awe, wondering how the human mind can see things that are not there and not see things that are clearly there. I never looked up how the sawing illusion is done. It is a classic, and I don't want to know. I don't want my surprise and amazement to be ruined.

Magicians direct and misdirect attention in ways that allow them to create illusions which seem impossible. Magic capitalizes on the failures of human observation and cognition.[28] Magic performances demonstrate that we do not "see" reality. In fact, cognitive scientists say that we only see what our minds have decided reality is, and our eyes can be easily deceived. Many famous experiments bear this out. Magicians use those failings of human observation and cognition to befuddle and surprise us.

So do politicians and other con men.

FLAWED RECALL

> *What we ... refer to confidently as memory ... is really a form of storytelling that ... often changes with the telling.*
> —William Maxwell, So Long, See You Tomorrow, 1980

Beyond our flawed perceptions of reality, we also have to deal with flawed recall.

Any study of memory is, in the main, a study of its frailty. In *Remember*, an engrossing survey of the latest memory research, Lisa Genova explains that a healthy brain quickly forgets most of what passes into conscious awareness. The fragments of experience that do get encoded into long-term memory are then subject to "creative editing." To remember an event is to reimagine it; in the reimagining, we inadvertently introduce new information, often colored by our current emotional state. A dream, a suggestion, and even the mere passage of time can warp a memory.

It is sobering to realize that three out of four prisoners who are later exonerated through DNA evidence were initially convicted on

---

[28] "When we see a magic trick, when something happens that seems impossible, we are forced to realize the limits of our views, our doubts, and our expectations." Jim Steinmeyer, quoted in Joshua Jay, *How Magicians Think*, 306.

the basis of eyewitness testimony. "You can be 100 percent confident in your vivid memory," Genova writes, "and still be 100 percent wrong."

Elizabeth Loftus, a professor at the University of California, Irvine, has made a career pulling aside the "flimsy curtain that separates our imagination and our memory." Loftus, in her research and books, has "obliterated the idea that there is a permanent stable memory capacity in humans."[29] She has testified, usually for the defense, in more than 300 cases on behalf of people who were, or may have been, wrongfully accused.

According to Loftus, "You can plant entire events [that never happened] into the minds of otherwise ordinary, healthy people." Experiments have established various means by which our memories can be hacked. Incredibly, people can even be induced to create false confessions to the commission of crimes that they did not commit, and could not possibly have committed.

Our brains are actually designed to fill in missing gaps in our memories with the imagination's own inventions. The embellishments are inevitably more entertaining and interesting than what may have actually happened. I have been accused of embellishing my stories, lying, and making things up, but that is just the way my brain (and yours, too) works.

The renowned Japanese film director Kurosawa made flawed perceptions and flawed recall the theme of his famous movie, *Rashomon*. In that film, four eyewitnesses recount different versions of a man's murder and the rape of his wife. The stories were wildly different from each other. The eyewitness problem is now so widely accepted that it is referred to by cognitive scientists as the "Rashomon Effect." Another good reason for police body cameras.

My childhood chronicle is a vivid example of the Rashomon effect. My brothers and I have radically different versions of events, and each of us is convinced that our version is the correct one.

---

[29] James Doyle, "How Elizabeth Loftus Changed the Meaning of Memory," *The New Yorker*, April 5, 2021.

POSTMODERN PHILOSOPHY

Apart from the twin problems of flawed perception and minds filled with false, unreliable, and contaminated memories, there is the deeper philosophical question of "What is reality anyway?" Some philosophers and intellectuals of the modern age, called by various names—relativists, postmodernists, and deconstructionists—argue that there is no objective reality at all waiting to be perceived.

David McRaney in *You Are Now Less Dumb* argues that "The last one hundred years of research suggest that you, and everyone else, still believe in a form of naïve realism. You still believe that, although your inputs may not be perfect, once you get to thinking and feeling, those thoughts and feelings are reliable and predictable. We now know that there is no way you can ever know an 'objective' reality, and we know that you can never know how much of subjective reality is a fabrication, because you never experience anything other than the output of your mind. Everything that's ever happened to you has happened inside your skull."

Albert Camus, a philosopher (who was baffling, like Kierkegaard), said: "A man defines himself by his make-believe as well as by his sincere impulses."[30]

QUANTUM PHYSICS AND SCHRÖDINGER'S CAT

To make the problem of perception, memory, and reality even more confusing, there is the quantum physics problem of what IS reality at any given time. According to some respected quantum mechanics experts, things (like small particles) can go both left and right at the same time, possibly in parallel universes.

The most disturbing thought experiment about this question of reality, especially if you are an animal lover, involves Schrödinger's cat. That is the peculiar idea, familiar to all quantum mechanics

---

[30] Albert Camus, "An Absurd Reasoning" (essay).

connoisseurs, that a cat in a box with a radioactive particle can be both dead and alive, depending on the observer. This is problematic for what we typically understand as external "reality."

PSYCHEDELIC EXPERIENCES

And then there are the alternate realities offered by psychedelics. Anyone who has experimented with LSD, psilocybin mushrooms, or peyote knows that one's normal understanding of reality is forever shattered once those chemicals have entered your brain. Aldous Huxley explained it all many years ago in his book, *Doors of Perception*, and many others have written about the alternate realities experienced under the influence of drugs, including, most recently, Michael Pollan in two books, *This is Your Mind on Plants* and *How to Change Your Mind*, the latter of which is also a documentary film series.

Admitting the illusions of perception, the slipperiness of memories, the postmodern philosophical denial of absolute truth, the confusing quantum physics questions about the nature of reality, and the alternate reality experienced by people on psychedelics, I persisted, nonetheless, in putting in this book what seem to me some of my most vivid memories. Whether they are true and real or not is a hopeless and meaningless quest.

Sorry about that.

ABOUT THE AUTHOR

The author, Pope Barrow

Pope Barrow was born in Savannah, Georgia, during World War II. After the war, the family moved to a farm in Maryland, where two brothers were added. Pope's future would be deeply influenced by the years he spent as an adventurous, largely unsupervised farm kid.

Pope attended Gilman, a private high school in Baltimore, and then Yale College and Harvard Law School, both on academic scholarships. Searching for a career out of the normal lawyer mold, he wound up in Washington, D.C., writing legislation for the U.S. House of Representatives.

In less than two years, Pope abandoned Washington on a quest to find the meaning of life. That search took him first to North Africa and then onto the so-called Hippie Trail, traveling overland from England to Nepal. His search was ultimately fruitless—but fun, adventurous, and a little reckless.

Back home, Pope returned to writing legislation for Congress and stayed nearly 40 years, ultimately advancing to head of the office. The quest for fun persisted, however. Outside of the office, Pope traveled to many parts of the world for whitewater kayaking and sought to protect whitewater rivers nationwide from development. Later he sailed the seas as crew on others' sailboats, eventually acquiring his own, which he cruised up and down the coast as far as New England and the Bahamas.

Pope has been married and divorced twice, and has three children and two grandchildren. For the last 20 years, he has lived with his soulmate, Amber Jones. Now in his 80s, despite a decade of struggle with cancer, he continues to race sailboats, dance, play pickleball, and farm a community garden plot. He perseveres in the pursuit of fun.

A sample of published writings describing the author's adventures and achievements:

David Brown, *The Whitewater Wars: The Rafters and the River Trip that Saved the Ocoee & The Gauley River Battle* (self-pub., 2020).

John Lancaster, "Why Would a Sane Person Do This? Because it's Fun," *The Washington Post Magazine*, February 28, 1988, 20-23.

Rob Schultheis, "Life on the Fall Line: World-class boating in the heart of the city," *Outside*, June 1985, 67-71.